Rachel Martino, MEd

Gifted and Talented Workbook for Kids

101

Engaging Activities to Nurture Budding Skills and Interests

AGES 5 TO 7

ROCKRIDGE PRESS

For general information on our other products and services or to obtain technical support, please contact our Customer Care Department within the United States at (866) 744-2665, or outside the United States at (510) 253-0500.

Rockridge Press publishes its books in a variety of electronic and print formats. Some content that appears in print may not be available in electronic books, and vice versa.

Interior and Cover Designer: Brieanna Felschow
Art Producer: Hannah Dickerson
Editor: Carolyn Abate
Production Editor: Rachel Taenzler
Production Manager: Riley Hoffman

Illustrations © 2021 Collaborate Agency
Author photo courtesy of Andrea Simon

Paperback ISBN: 978-1-64876-724-1
eBook ISBN: 978-1-64876-556-8
R1

I dedicate this book to my third grade
teacher, Mrs. Hammond.
Thank you for inspiring me to be
the teacher I am today.

Contents

Introduction

Hi! I am Rachel Martino, an educator passionate about meeting the unique needs of gifted students and challenging them to reach their fullest potential. I myself was considered a gifted child, so I have a firsthand understanding of the struggles, challenges, and limitations that gifted students may face in the classroom setting. As a teacher and author, I create easy-to-implement resources for teachers to use in their classroom to challenge and engage their gifted learners. However, before writing this book, one very important piece of the puzzle was missing—I had no outlet for providing tips and resources for the parents of gifted children. This book will help you understand your gifted (or potentially gifted) child even more, will show you what gifted education may look like, and provides you with 101 exercises and activities to challenge your child at home. By becoming educated on this topic and having the tools and resources to meet your child's needs, you can become a powerful supporter and advocate for your child.

Before we dive in, let's make sure that this book is exactly what you are looking for. Because of your child's age range (five to seven), there is a good chance your child hasn't yet been tested or even identified as "Gifted and Talented." So, let's take a quick look about what it means to be gifted. A gifted child is one who shows the potential for achieving higher than their peers in many areas beyond just academics. Creativity and leadership abilities are also considered. Gifted education, and even gifted identification, varies from state to state and school district to school district. We'll dive into what it could look like in the introduction of this book.

While the exercises and activities in this workbook develop skills that children may need when taking gifted identification assessments, the main purpose of this book isn't purely to provide test prep. Rather, this book is perfect for any parent who believes their child may be gifted, or a parent who simply wants to provide their curious child with intellectually and creatively stimulating exercises and activities. With a wide range of exercises and activities ranging from critical thinking to language arts and math, hands-on science, and even creativity, you and your child are sure to engage in some really fun learning! Spending a little bit of time on this workbook each week will build your child's skills in academic subjects, creativity, and critical thinking.

For Parents: Gifted Education, This Workbook, and You

In this section, I will provide you with guidance on how to use this book. I will also share an overview of, and insight on, Gifted and Talented education, including what it looks like, challenges, common traits of gifted children, and more. You'll also find an informal assessment that can help you determine if your child might be gifted.

What Exactly Is Gifted and Talented Education?

Gifted and Talented education is a broad term that describes a specialized program, instructional approach, or instructional strategy that takes place in the school setting. The focus is on serving, challenging, and meeting the unique needs of children identified as Gifted and Talented. This is through academic support or outlets for creativity and social-emotional support. Some schools have separate, dedicated gifted programs and services, while others may integrate gifted education and differentiation into the regular classroom.

There are two main methods or approaches found in schools: enrichment and acceleration. One approach is not significantly better than the other. However, most schools format their gifted program to fit their school's population.

Enrichment activities are focused on creativity, critical thinking, social-emotional needs, and research projects based on student choice. Students can be assigned additional activities in the classroom or be pulled out of the class and work with a special group for a set amount of time each week.

Acceleration allows for the education concepts and activities to be increased to match your child's quicker learning pace. It usually occurs when a child easily masters concepts at their grade level or if a student catches on to concepts much more quickly than their peers.

IN THE CLASSROOM

When entering kindergarten, it is highly unlikely for any child to already be identified as gifted. That first year is really about students getting comfortable with being in a school setting. Your child's teacher is focused on getting to know each student by observing their individual traits and academic strengths and weaknesses.

One of the best practices in gifted education is to give students opportunities to interact with their gifted peers, study with their mixed-ability peers, and explore topics on their own. This is called cluster grouping. If your child's school has multiple classes per grade level, gifted students are likely grouped together along with other mixed-ability peers to make up an entire class. Clustering allows the teacher to differentiate students without any of them becoming overlooked.

This is more common in the lower grades when fewer students, if any, are already identified. Gifted education tends to ramp up as students get older, through either an acceleration or enrichment model.

OUTSIDE OF SCHOOL

Outside of school, there are few opportunities designed specifically for gifted enrichment and education for students aged five to seven. That doesn't mean there aren't ways to support your child outside of school, but you will likely have to spend some time figuring out your options.

If you have the resources, allow your child to take classes that align with their interests. These could include music, art, dance, and more. Science, STEM, and robotics kits and activities give your child some hands-on experience in these fields. Another option is to seek other like-minded children to create a club that aligns with their interests. The local library is also a great source for finding books that feed those interests.

Because gifted education for five-to-seven-year-olds will take place mainly at home, it's important to follow your child's lead. Follow their interests and let them determine how much time to spend on something.

THE CHALLENGES FACING GIFTED EDUCATION

Inequity and inequality are unfortunately seen across the board, in all aspects of education. Gifted education is no different. The achievement gap between students who come from a minority, low-income, or non-English language learning background and nonminority and higher income students is wide. Students who come from these populations are underrepresented in gifted education, but the education community is working to remedy this issue.

Nonverbal tests that employ shapes and pictures are increasing in popularity to combat this testing gap. They allow educators to assess the reasoning and critical thinking skill of a potentially gifted student, even if English isn't their first language.

Universal screening is another approach to address inequity within the gifted education community. Testing all students provides more opportunity for everyone. By using multiple measures and data points, we are more likely to identify a broader group of children. However, some schools only rely on teacher referrals for student testing and assessments.

Additionally, screening all students as they move into higher grades may give time for some to catch up to their peers.

Who Qualifies as "Gifted"?

According to the Elementary and Secondary Education Act, a gifted student is defined as:

> *Students, children, or youth who give evidence of high achievement capability in areas such as intellectual, creative, artistic, or leadership capacity, or in specific academic fields, and who need services and activities not ordinarily provided by the school in order to fully develop those capabilities.*

For Parents: Gifted Education, This Workbook, and You

In simpler terms, a child qualifies as gifted if they show that they are capable of achieving on a higher level than their peers in many categories, both intellectual and academic, along with creativity and leadership.

The US Department of Education Office for Civil Rights estimates that 6 percent of public school students are identified as gifted. Students can begin to be identified as young as six or seven years old, but they should be looked at beyond that age range because different kids mature and grow at different rates. An informal assessment on page xii will help you answer the question, "Is my child gifted?"

GIFTED TESTING 101

Just like the definition of "gifted," the methods and procedures for testing vary state by state, and school district by school district. In most cases, each school district has their own screening protocol for identifying gifted students.

Although the specific methods and procedures differ across the country, there are some constants and best practices to look for if your child is a candidate for assessment. Both objective and subjective measures should be taken, and identification should be based on multiple data points. Creativity, outside-of-the-box thinking, and problem-solving should be front and center, along with a student's leadership abilities and other traits that align with giftedness.

If you suspect that your child may be gifted, the first thing you should do is reach out to your child's teacher for more information on your school's identification process. At the school district I work at in Texas, we've always accepted parent requests for testing. However, we only accept them during our testing window.

WHAT ARE GIFTED TESTS DESIGNED TO ASSESS?

Gifted tests are designed to assess cognition, academic performance, and subjective measures that look at specific traits and behaviors that may suggest giftedness. We want to see *how* the child thinks, and not just what they know. Are they strong problem-solvers? Do they have good reasoning abilities?

Common IQ tests—The gold standard for assessing a child's gifted abilities are IQ tests that measure cognitive and intellectual abilities.

- **Stanford-Binet**—One of the most widely used IQ tests, the Stanford-Binet measures intelligence through reasoning, knowledge, visual-spatial processing, and memory.

- **NNAT (Naglieri Nonverbal Ability Test)**—This nonverbal test seeks to close the inequity gap between students with limited English proficiency and those who are native English speakers. It uses visuals such as puzzles and images to assess students' thinking and problem-solving abilities (*how* students think and reason), rather than measuring *what* the student knows.

CogAT—The Cognitive Abilities Test, or CogAT, assesses a student's reasoning and cognitive abilities in relation to those of their same-aged peers. There are verbal and nonverbal sections, along with a quantitative assessment looking at things such as number puzzles and analogies. The CogAT is not an IQ test.

Academic achievement—These tests measure whether the child is performing at a more advanced level as compared to their grade-level peers. One of the most common academic achievement tests is the Screening Assessment for Gifted Elementary and Middle School Students (SAGES). It assesses a student's abilities in math, science, language arts, and social studies, along with a section to assess reasoning and problem-solving.

Subjective assessments—Oftentimes, teachers and parents complete a subjective assessment to provide insight on a child's traits in and out of the classroom. The assessment in "Is My Child Gifted?" (page xii) is similar to a traits and behaviors assessment. These types of assessments vary between school districts, but they typically look at similar traits.

To build the commonly tested skills of problem-solving and reasoning, check out chapter 2. There you will find a host of reasoning and critical thinking activities. To prepare your child for the SAGES, all chapters in this book will be beneficial.

SHOULD I GET MY CHILD TESTED?

At this age, it's helpful to simply expose children to rich experiences and challenge them with activities and exercises like those found in this book. Nurture and foster problem-solving skills. Focus on providing rich experiences for your child. Most importantly, don't push them or overwhelm them with test prep or a lot of extra work. Follow their lead and explore things that they show interest in. They will learn so much just from day-to-day experiences and exposure to other people and children.

However, if you feel strongly that you want your child tested, hold on to that desire. Inquire at your child's school to get a better understanding of their process. Express to your child's teacher what specific traits and behaviors you see in your child; ask for their input. Together the two of you can come up with a plan.

COMMON TRAITS OF GIFTED CHILDREN

There are certain traits that may serve as a sign that your child may be gifted. Do they often exhibit outside-of-the-box thinking? Can they quickly solve problems without assistance? Do they consider creative solutions when problem-solving?

Even if your child exhibits some of these traits, it's important to make the distinction between a *smart* child and a *gifted* child. A smart child quickly picks up on new things, may be a high achiever in school, and likely loves to learn. They are usually well-behaved in class and enjoy completing all their school work. A smart child is identified based on *what* they know.

A gifted child is identified based on *how* they think, and not just *what* they know. Gifted children are not always high achievers. They often only engage in something that they are interested in. If they aren't adequately challenged, they may show disruptive behavior issues in the classroom or simply refuse to do their school work—this may be a sign that they are ahead of their peers or grade-level standard and are simply bored.

As a teacher of the Gifted and Talented students, I've come across a number of common traits that parents need to be aware of, which go beyond their academic abilities.

For Parents: Gifted Education, This Workbook, and You

Gifted children tend to skew anxious. These children are often more aware of what's going on around them. They also tend to think things through at a deeper level. This can cause anxiety because these children can overthink things and worry.

Perfectionism is a common characteristic. At first glance, you may think this is a strength. However, this trait may cause a child to feel like they are never good enough, or they may refuse to move on from a task until they feel like it is perfect. Praising the process and not the end product can help children with this trait.

Gifted students are likely to become intensely interested in one subject or topic. They may want to study and learn all there is to know about it. On the flip side, gifted students may have a hard time engaging when they are not interested in a topic.

Boredom can lead to low grades and behavior issues in the classroom. Gifted students who haven't been academically challenged may get really frustrated and give up when they encounter something challenging or something that doesn't align with their interests.

A gifted child asks a lot of deep and thoughtful questions. They may inquire about how things work, or why things are the way they are. Gifted children may also be able to provide details, examples, and comparisons to explain things and illustrate their point.

Is My Child Gifted?

• • • • • • • • • • • • • • • • • • • •

Remember, testing varies from state to state, but this is a good baseline to see whether your child is exhibiting any gifted traits.

Format: 1–5 scale on the following traits (1= my child never demonstrates this trait, 5=my child always demonstrates this trait)

If you score your child a 4 or 5, try to think of specific examples that support that score. Is it a trait they demonstrate every day, multiple times a day?

_____ **My child has deep interests in very specific topics and desires to know everything about them**

_____ **My child is able to quickly solve problems on their own, often with creative solutions**

_____ **My child gets frustrated or disinterested when faced with a task that is too challenging**

_____ **My child gets disinterested/disengaged when faced with a topic they aren't interested in**

_____ **My child asks a lot of deeper-level thinking/thoughtful questions**

_____ **My child is great at communicating for their age, and can provide details, examples, and specific scenarios to illustrate their point**

_____ **My child creates unique things out of common objects**

_____ My child easily picks up on humor and/or sarcasm

_____ My child quickly understands new concepts, and is able to make connections between new things and things they've learned before

_____ My child is highly focused, engaged, and hardworking when completing self-selected tasks

If you scored your child a 4 or 5 on at least half of these measures, your child is showing traits that align with those found in gifted children. We use a similar assessment in my school district to measure these traits in our students.

About the Activities in This Book

The activities in this book are designed to engage and challenge your child. They cover five main categories. Part 1 features on-the-page exercises focused on language arts, reasoning and critical thinking, and math. Part 2 features many off-the-page activities and projects to get students more hands-on in the areas of creativity and science.

Each activity features instructions for the child, as well as a tip for you, the parent, to support your child in completing the activity. Some activities include creative writing, analogies, simple logic puzzles, patterns, and so much more. Some activities will be easy for your child to tackle, while others may pose a greater challenge. There are a few similar activities that get progressively harder, while others are independent, stand-alone activities.

You will need some materials to complete the activities and exercises in this book, including colored pencils, markers, and crayons. You'll be asked to collect items from nature or household materials. Be sure to review each exercise for its list of materials before you get started.

WHERE TO START

This following table outlines which activities and exercises may assist in familiarizing your child with activities related to those that may be found in specific gifted assessments. While the focus of this book is to build your child's abilities overall, exposure to these activities may help prepare your child in gifted assessments they may take in the future.

ASSESSMENT	EXERCISES AND ACTIVITIES
Stanford-Binet IQ Test	All activities in this book
NNAT	All activities in chapter 2
CogAT	All activities in chapter 2, and specific activities in chapter 3: Completing Carla's Patterns Martin's Missing Numbers Dominic's Dominoes Geometry All Around Me
SAGES	All activities in chapters 1 to 3 and 5
Subjective Assessments to Identify Traits, Attributes, and Behaviors	All activities in chapters 2 and 4

Before You Begin

· · · · · · · · · · · · · · · · ·

I can't wait for you to see your child blossom, explore, gain confidence, and find new interests through the activities and exercises in this workbook. There's really not one right way to complete this book. But to make the most out of this book, I suggest the following tips and pointers:

1. Let your child pick activities and exercises they are interested in.

2. Follow your child's lead during the activities and exercises. Let them be creative and explore; the exact directions of each exercise aren't important.

3. Spend only a little bit of time on this book each day or each week.

4. Keep in mind that children can be gifted in different areas, so there may be one chapter in which your child isn't strong.

5. Don't force the workbook onto your child; this should be a fun experience.

6. Provide plenty of praise and encouragement.

7. Meaningful sharing is important; FaceTime a grandparent to share an exercise they did.

8. Most of all, just have fun with it!

PART 1

Exercises, Puzzles, and Games

This section features on-the-page activities including exercises, puzzles, and games that are designed to be fun and engaging for your child. These activities are broken into three chapters: Language Arts, Reasoning and Critical Thinking, and Math. Your child can pick and choose the activities within these chapters. They don't have to be completed in a specific order.

CHAPTER 1

Language Arts

Language arts are skills such as spelling, reading, and writing. They help you share your ideas using language or words. This chapter is full of activities and exercises that will help you practice writing sentences, learn new words, make up stories, and more! You can pick the activities you want to do—and in any order you like.

All about Me

Directions: Are you funny? Shy? Tall or short? What color is your hair? These words are called characteristics! Think of five characteristics you have. Write them in the box. Then draw a picture of each characteristic. Do you know anybody who has these characteristics, too?

PARENT CORNER: This activity will encourage your child to self-reflect and practice identifying character traits by using themself as the subject. I suggest you let your child come up with their own descriptive words. You can prompt them by asking questions about how they are in different situations. For example, "How do you act when you are with Grandma?" This will help your child think about themself in these real-life scenarios and determine their character.

Goal-Getter

Directions: Setting goals is a great way to challenge yourself and to grow your brain. Think about something you've always wanted to do—ride your bike without falling down or learn to make your bed all by yourself. Write one of your goals inside each of the stars.

PARENT CORNER: Goal-setting can help your child develop focus, purpose, and drive. If your child is having trouble coming up with goals, share one of your goals with them. To make this activity even more meaningful, share a positive story about a time when you achieved a goal and how it made you feel.

Passion Exploration

Directions: What is something that you *really* like to do and learn about? Maybe you really like doing math problems or spending all day kicking a soccer ball. Write that thing on the line next to the word *topic*. For example, let's say you want to learn to cook. Write that as the topic. Then make a list of things you already know how to cook, such as a grilled cheese sandwich. In the next column, write down things you want to learn, such as pancakes or pizza.

Topic: _____

WHAT I ALREADY KNOW	WHAT I WANT TO LEARN

PARENT CORNER: Gifted children tend to really dive into topics that they are passionate about, so this activity works well with that frame of mind. To make a personal connection with your child, share one of your passions. For more inspiration, go to the library, look online, or use books you already have to read with your child about a topic they are passionate about. See if you can find some resources together to help your child learn the skills they mentioned in their chart.

Picture to Word Search

Directions: Farmer Fred has lost some items on his farm. Can you help him find them? The pictures are all the items he lost. Look for the word for each item in the grid to help Farmer Fred find them.

A	E	O	A	H
C	A	K	E	G
A	E	N	S	A
T	C	A	P	G
S	O	M	O	S
V	W	D	O	G
H	E	V	N	R
M	O	U	S	E
E	A	H	E	P

Answers on page 128.

PARENT CORNER: This activity gets your child thinking about *how* to spell the words before looking for them in the word search. If your child is having trouble, start by asking them to say the word that the picture represents. If they are unsure how to spell it, encourage them to sound it out or help them look for the first letter of each word and go from there.

What's Your Story?

Directions: It's story time—and you are going to write the story! This is your chance to use your wildest imagination. First, draw a picture in the box. Next, give your picture a title. Now write a fun story about the picture on the lines below. How creative can you get?

_____

_____

_____

_____

_____

PARENT CORNER: This open-ended exercise challenges your child to write without parameters and lets them really explore themself as a writer. This type of writing mirrors popular instructional methods that teachers use in the classroom. By first drawing a picture, your child starts with a reference to help them develop their story with specific details. If your child has trouble coming up with a topic, encourage them to start drawing and go from there.

Tall, Taller, Tallest

Directions: Have you ever seen these animals before in pictures or in real life? Are they all the same size or are they different? On the line underneath each animal, write the word *tall*, *taller*, or *tallest*. You should use each word only once. Then come up with three new things that are tall, taller, and tallest. Draw them in the boxes.

_____   _____   _____

Tall	Taller	Tallest

Answers on page 128.

PARENT CORNER: This activity focuses on comparative terms—which can be tricky for kids—but sets up your child for success. By first analyzing a given example, kids are able to learn the concept of these comparative terms. Then they get a chance to apply this knowledge by creating their own examples. Creation requires your child to use more advanced thinking skills.

Creature Comparisons

Directions: In the last activity, we used three words to compare and describe different animals: tall, taller, and tallest. There are many other words we can use compare things. Take a look at the animals. How many words can you use to compare them? If you need help, use the word bank. Fill in the words that describe each animal in the box below it.

WORD BANK			
Tall	Fast	Smelly	Loud
Taller	Faster	Smellier	Louder
Tallest	Fastest	Smelliest	Loudest

PARENT CORNER: This activity builds on the previous one. By encouraging your child to come up with their own comparative terms, you are enabling them to apply higher-order thinking. As long as your child can explain their reasoning for their choices, praise them even if you don't agree with the comparative terms they selected. They may see things differently than you do.

Story Misprint

Directions: Someone wrote a story on the computer, but when they printed it out some of the words disappeared! We need your help to figure out what the writer wanted to say. Fill in each blank with a word to complete the story.

Once upon a _____, there were three _____.
The _____ all loved playing outside, and they all loved
sports. Each one had a favorite _____. The oldest one loved
to play _____. The middle one loved to play _____.
The youngest one's favorite sport was _____. Whenever
they played their favorite sports, they always _____. They were
very _____. One day, their _____ encouraged
them to try a new sport together. They tried playing _____,
but they were so _____. After that, they each decided to
stick with their favorite sports. They lived _____ ever after.

What Do You Think?

Directions: If you saw a friend crying on the playground at school, what would you think about them? Would you think they are sad or hurt? Why is that? Because you know that when people cry, it's usually because they're sad or hurt. Look at the picture, then answer the questions to figure out what the picture is saying.

What do you see? _____

_____

What do you think? _____

_____

What makes you think that? _____

_____

Based on what you wrote above, what do you understand about this picture? _____

_____

PARENT CORNER: Making inferences is a key higher-order thinking skill that is found in all academic subjects, but mainly language arts. It helps students get more from what they are reading. They learn to use information in the text to make educated guesses about a character's motivation, or how a character feels. This skill also has real-world applications. When your child is making inferences, ask them to explain what makes them think that. What do they see in the picture or what do they know from prior knowledge that makes them think that?

Everyday Emotions

Directions: Every day, you have many different feelings or emotions. Sometimes you may wake up happy, but as the day goes on, you might feel angry or sad. People often don't realize it, but their feelings often show up on their faces. Take a look at the kids' faces. How is each child feeling? What do you think made them feel that way? Write your answers on the lines.

What is the child feeling?

_____ _____ _____

What do you think made them feel this way?

_____ _____ _____

What is the child feeling?

_____ _____ _____

What do you think made them feel this way?

_____ _____ _____

Answers on page 129.

PARENT CORNER: Learning to make inferences about emotions will allow your child to reach a deeper level of comprehension in the books they are reading. It also boosts their communication skills and builds their empathy and understanding of others. If your child has trouble identifying the emotions in an image, encourage them to think about what makes them feel the way that child looks. Creating that personal experience can help them make an inference about the child in the picture.

Create Cal's Story

Directions: Cal heard that you are a very creative storyteller, so he's asking you for some help. He spent a lot of time drawing a picture. Now he would like a fun and exciting story to go with it! You are the perfect person for the job. Take a look at his drawing. Use the lines underneath to write a creative story to go with it.

_____

_____

_____

PARENT CORNER: This activity may be challenging for your child because they have to come up with a creative story that aligns with someone else's drawing. Oftentimes, it's easy to come up with a story for one's own drawings. This exercise will inspire your child to analyze the drawing and think about the perspective of the child who drew it.

It's Easy as A to Z

Directions: Put on your thinking cap! In this exercise, I challenge you to come up with one word that starts with each letter of the alphabet. If you get stuck on a letter, it's okay to skip it and come back to it later. Was that too easy? Try coming up with words that are all animals, food, or things in nature!

PARENT CORNER: This activity gets your child thinking about spelling and connecting the alphabet to things they know. If your child is having trouble coming up with a word for some of the letters, encourage them to look around the room and name the objects around them. Alternatively, pick a category such as animals or food to encourage them to come up with words.

Dinner Details

Directions: Writing a story with lots of details takes practice. When you're writing a story, a good way to come up with details is to think about your five senses—sight, smell, taste, touch, and hearing. This can help you think about how to describe things. Tonight, when you eat dinner, think about how your dinner looks, tastes, smells, feels, and sounds. When dinner is over, write down the things you notice.

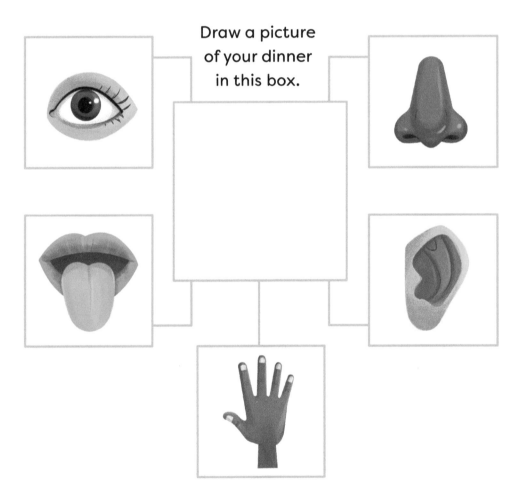

Draw a picture of your dinner in this box.

PARENT CORNER: By using the five senses strategy, your child will gain a tangible skill that they can apply to any writing they do in the future. While your child is completing this exercise, encourage them to focus and get as descriptive as possible.

Just Right for Me

Directions: To get the most fun out of reading, it's important to know how to find a book that is not too easy, but not too difficult to read. The Just Right Rule helps you figure that out. When you find a book you want to read, look at the instructions. Start at the bottom of the ladder and follow the directions in number order to figure out if that book is "just right" for you!

4. If you passed the top of the ladder, this book may not be a good fit for you just yet!

3. If you went up three to five rungs, this book should be just the right fit for you!

2. If you went up fewer than two rungs, this book might be too easy.

1. Pick a book that looks interesting to you. Open to any page and begin reading. Each time you get to a word you don't understand, climb up one rung of the ladder. How many rungs did you climb?

PARENT CORNER: The Just Right Rule will help your child grow as a reader by helping them pick books that are not too easy, but can still be read successfully. This activity will work best if you have a variety of books at different reading levels for your child to look at. You may have plenty of books at home to complete this activity. Alternatively, you can take your child to the library, where there will be more than enough books to choose from!

Fun Free Writing

Directions: Do you have a story inside you that is just waiting to come out? This is your chance to have fun with creative writing! Use the lines on this page to write it out. It can be a true story, or something totally made up! When you're done, talk to a parent about your story and how you came up with it.

_____

_____

_____

_____

_____

_____

_____

_____

PARENT CORNER: The goal of this exercise is to foster your child's writing ability and interest in writing. Let your child tell you about the story. Ask questions to help them with the process: How did you get the idea to write about that? When you picture the story your head, what other details do you see? Can you sound out the word?

Directions: Today, you will create your very own comic strip! There are two ways to do this. You can use the characters and important events from your favorite book to make your comic, or you can make up your own story and characters. It's up to you. The only goal is to have fun with your creation!

Title _____

PARENT CORNER: This activity will benefit your child no matter which direction they choose. If they use their favorite book, they will need to identify key ideas and important details from that story to create their comic. If they create their own comic, they will use their creativity and imagination to put together a story. If they aren't sure where to start, look at some kid-friendly comics to give them some ideas.

Look at My Favorite Book!

Directions: Think about all the books you have read. Which is your absolute favorite? Since you love that book so much, the author wants you to create a poster to help more people learn about it! Use the box for your poster. Make sure you include the title of the book, the author, and drawings or words to explain why this book is so good.

PARENT CORNER: This fun activity is about creating a persuasive piece of art about a book your child loves. If they can't pick just one favorite book, have them make additional posters on other pieces of paper. Encourage them to add lots of details.

It's Rhyme Time

Directions: Ready, Freddy? Let's rhyme! Words that rhyme are words that end with the same sound. Take a look at the first table. Can you find which pairs of words rhyme and which don't? In the second table, come up with your own rhyming pairs. Time to rhyme!

WORD ONE	WORD TWO	DO THEY RHYME? YES / NO
Cat	Hat	
Muffin	Puffin	
Drill	Drum	
Jewel	Cool	

Answers on page 129.

Fill in the next table with three sets of rhyming words.

WORD ONE	WORD TWO

PARENT CORNER: This activity builds your child's understanding of rhyme. Identifying words that rhyme increases their confidence and their reading and speaking abilities. When your child creates their own list of rhyming words, they use their higher-order thinking. If your child is having trouble, encourage them to say each word aloud to determine which ones rhyme.

Verb, Noun, or Neither?

Directions: A verb is an action word. It's something that you can do! A noun is a person, place, or thing. Draw a box around each verb, then circle each noun. Be careful! There are three trick words that aren't verbs or nouns! See if you can find the three trick words, then cross them out.

Run	Puppy	Under	Penguin
Jump	Pretty	Mouse	School
Dog	Horse	Bedroom	Desk
Crawl	Monkey	Chair	Quickly

Answers on page 129.

PARENT CORNER: This activity helps strengthen your child's ability to identify nouns and verbs by including three trick words. Since trick words are in the mix, your child will have to critically and closely analyze each word before determining what it might be. This is a great way to reinforce the concepts and definitions of these parts of speech, and will help them develop a deeper understanding of each.

Gifted and Talented Workbook for Kids

Amazing Adjectives

Directions: Adjectives are words that describe a noun. Slimy, cold, and blue are all adjectives. When you use adjectives in your writing, you help your reader imagine the scene or person you are talking about in your story. Let's practice using adjectives to describe this tiger. Look at the picture. Then write one adjective on each of the six lines around it.

_____   _____

_____   _____

_____   _____

PARENT CORNER: By now, your child should know what a noun is. This activity will challenge them to build on that knowledge by practicing descriptions of a noun. It is a great way to encourage your child to use more detail and descriptive words. This skill will take their creative writing to the next level. If your child is having trouble coming up with adjectives, ask them to look closely at the picture and tell you what they see.

CHAPTER 2

Reasoning and Critical Thinking

This chapter involves your thinking skills. These types of skills help you understand ideas, problem-solve, and make sense of the information around you. The exercises in this chapter will make you think. They may be challenging at first, but once you get the hang of it, you will find these activities are a lot of fun!

What Comes Next?

Directions: It's time to be a detective! The rows of shapes are missing their final pieces. To figure out what the missing pieces should be, you will need to figure out the pattern of shapes for each row. Look closely at each shape and think about how it is positioned. Then decide what shape should go at the end. Draw that final shape on the line.

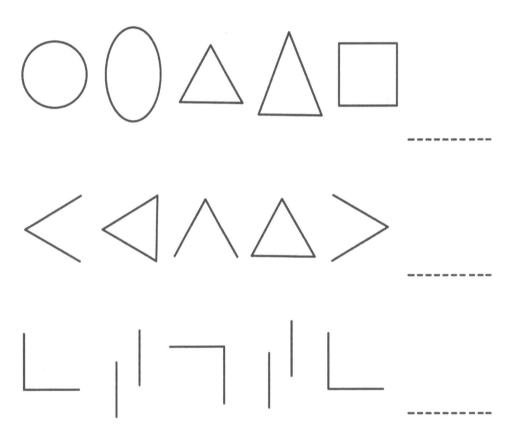

Answers on page 130.

PARENT CORNER: This exercise is a great way to sharpen your child's critical thinking skills. Each series in this exercise is designed to be progressively harder. If your child is having trouble, walk them through one shape at a time. Ask them how the second shape is different from the first, then how the third shape is different from the second, and so on until they figure out the pattern in that series.

Create Your Own Pattern

Directions: Patterns are all around you. Make your own patterns right on this page! Create three sets of different patterns on the lines. You can draw pictures, write numbers, or use colors to create your pattern. Your idea can be simple, or it can be complex. It is up to you to create the patterns you want!

1. _____

2. _____

3. _____

1. _____

2. _____

3. _____

PARENT CORNER: This exercise engages your child in higher-order thinking skills by having them create their own patterns. This exercise is open-ended to allow your child to explore and create what they want. However, if they create one or two very simple patterns, encourage them to make the next more complex.

Parallel Patterns

Directions: For each pattern given, create a parallel pattern on the line below it. A parallel uses the same rules as the first pattern. In the example, you can see that the original pattern was circle, oval, circle, oval, etc. The parallel pattern is square, rectangle, square, rectangle, etc. Try making parallel patterns for numbers 2 and 3!

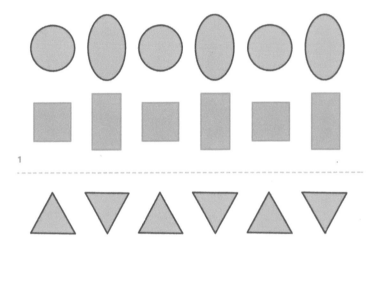

1

2

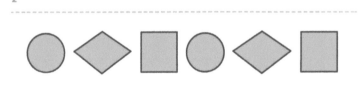

3

PARENT CORNER: This exercise gives your child the chance to use what they learned from the previous pattern exercises to create new patterns based on the ones pictured. There is likely more than one correct parallel pattern for each. If you aren't sure about your child's answer, have them explain to you how their pattern is similar to the one given to them.

Gifted and Talented Workbook for Kids

Pattern Perfector

Directions: You have the power to make these patterns perfect! Take a close look at each pattern. Try to figure out what is missing in each line. For each puzzle, draw the missing shape to complete the patterns.

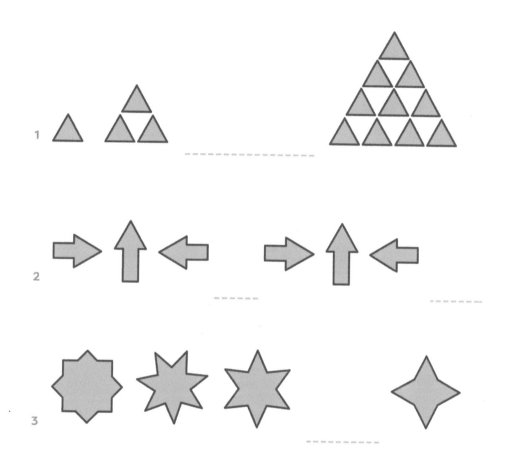

Answers on page 130.

PARENT CORNER: This exercise resembles those that might be found in common gifted assessments. If your child hasn't seen patterns like these before, they may be overwhelmed with this exercise. You may want to cover up the bottom two patterns with a blank piece of paper while your child works on the first one. That way they can concentrate on figuring out one pattern at a time.

Peter's Pattern Problem

Directions: Help! Peter tried to make some patterns, but he accidentally included one shape in each row that doesn't belong. You can help Peter by crossing out the shape in each row that ruins the pattern. With your help, Peter's pattern problem can be solved. Perfect!

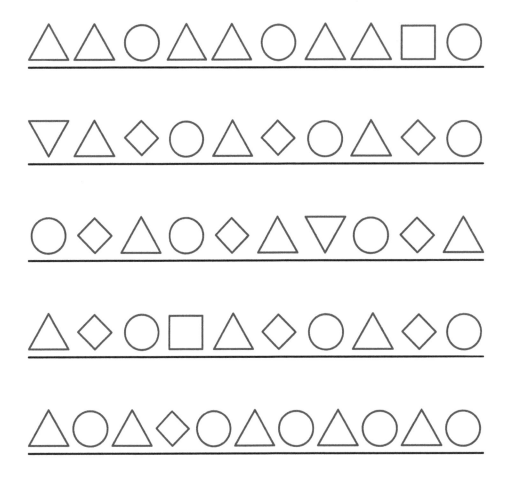

Answers on page 131.

PARENT CORNER: Rather than just asking your child to identify if something is a pattern or not, this exercise makes them analyze *why* a group is not a pattern. If your child is having trouble figuring this out, you can help them by encouraging them to determine what the pattern is supposed to be. Try saying the names of the shapes out loud to identify the odd one out.

Max's Car Collection

Directions: Max has a special collection of toy cars. He has five cars in all. Each car is a different color: red, blue, yellow, orange, and green. Max wants to line them up a certain way, and he needs your help. Read the instructions Max gave you to figure out the order in which to put his cars. There are two different ways you can line up the cars following Max's directions.

1. Max does not want his cars to be lined up in rainbow order.

2. Max wants the blue car to be on one end, and the green car to be on the other.

3. Max wants his red, yellow, and orange cars to be lined up in alphabetical order.

Use the space to figure out an order for Max's car collection.

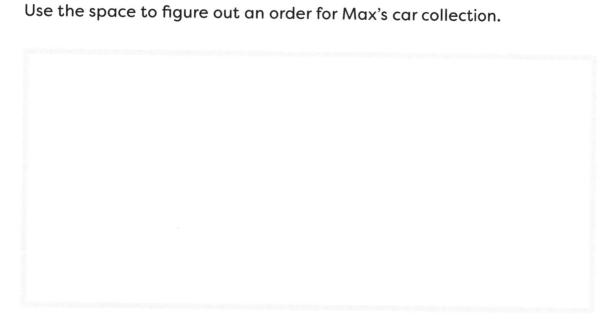

Answers on page 131.

PARENT CORNER: This activity is a great introduction to logic puzzles. The order of Max's cars needs to meet all three criteria that he outlined. If your child creates a combination that only meets one or two of the criteria, encourage them to look back at the one or two they haven't met. Then ask them what they can do to meet all the criteria.

Super School Subjects

Directions: Jessica, Jamal, and Jeremy are in the same class. Their teacher knows that they each have a different favorite subject, but she doesn't know what they are. Use the clues to help their teacher figure out each student's favorite subject. The table will help you keep track of the clues so you can solve the puzzle.

Clue 1 tells us that Jessica does not like math so there's an X in the box next to her name, under the math column. Remember that each child has a different favorite subject, so each subject can't be loved by more than one of the children.

Jessica, Jamal, and Jeremy all have a different favorite school subject.

1. Jessica does not like math.
2. Jamal loves his favorite subject because he likes doing experiments.
3. Jeremy's favorite subject is not science.

	MATH	READING	SCIENCE
Jessica	X		
Jamal			
Jeremy			

Answers on page 131.

PARENT CORNER: Logic puzzles are fun, and are especially popular for challenging gifted students. But it does take some practice to get the hang of how they work. If you aren't familiar with logic puzzles, take a peek at the answer key to see how these tables are typically marked. Essentially, an X goes into a box when the clues have helped you determine its combination is definitely not the answer. A circle (or check mark) goes in the boxes that are definitely true.

How Many Birthday Candles?

Directions: Three kids are having birthday parties at the park. Each kid is turning a different age. Use the clues and the grid to help the adults figure out how many candles should go on each kid's birthday cake. If you need help remembering how to use the grid, check out the instructions on page 32.

Maggie, Miguel, and Micah are each turning a different age.

1. Maggie is not the oldest of the three children.
2. Micah is the youngest.
3. Miguel needs more than six candles on his cake.

	5	6	7
Maggie			
Miguel			
Micah			

Answers on page 131.

PARENT CORNER: This exercise will help your child become more familiar and comfortable with logic puzzles. Once they've mastered the basic concepts and how they work, they can engage in higher-level logic puzzles. These puzzles engage your child's critical thinking and problem-solving skills. They also encourage your child to analyze and evaluate a set of clues to determine the solution.

Shape Sudoku 1

Directions: Sudoku is a special type of puzzle from Japan. You will need to use critical thinking and problem-solving skills to figure them out. To complete this sudoku, fill in each blank box with a shape. Each shape can appear only once in each row and each column. You may not get the answers right the first time. Use a pencil for this puzzle so you can erase if you make a mistake.

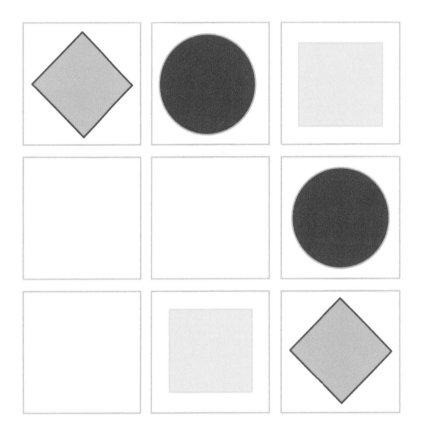

Answer on page 132.

PARENT CORNER: Sudoku puzzles are a fun way to get your child to practice critical thinking and problem-solving. These puzzles traditionally use numbers. Using shapes instead of numbers will help your child get used to—and succeed—at this type of puzzle. It's much easier for your child to picture how to complete the puzzle with a visual element.

Shape Sudoku 2

Directions: Let's exercise your new super sudoku skills with another shape puzzle! Fill in the blank boxes in the puzzle. Remember, each shape appears only once in each row and column. It's always a good idea to use a pencil for sudoku puzzles.

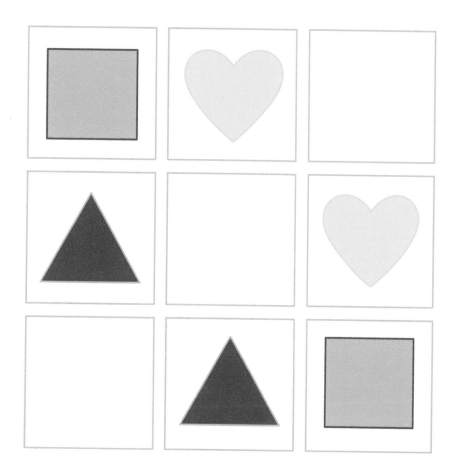

Answer on page 132.

PARENT CORNER: The more your child practices sudoku, the more comfortable they will get with how the puzzle works. Once they have the hang of it, they can move on to number sudoku. You'll find two number sudoku puzzles on the next two pages of this workbook.

Number Sudoku 1

Directions: You've had some good practice with sudoku puzzles. Ready to try another? This sudoku puzzle is a little different than the last two. It uses numbers instead of pictures. It works the same way though! Fill in the blank boxes so that each number (1, 2, and 3) appears only once in each row and column.

	1	2
1		3
2		1

Answer on page 132.

PARENT CORNER: The previous two puzzles featured shapes to help your child visualize how to solve this type of puzzle. Once they've mastered those, they should be able to do this traditional number sudoku puzzle with limited assistance.

Gifted and Talented Workbook for Kids

Number Sudoku 2

Directions: This the last sudoku puzzle! Fill in the blank boxes so that each number (1, 2, and 3) appears only once in each row and column. This one is a little more difficult, so take your time!

1		2
3		
2		3

Answer on page 132.

PARENT CORNER: By now, your child should be a sudoku puzzle master if they've completed the previous three puzzles. If your child really loves this type of puzzle, you can find plenty of them to print out for free online for more sudoku puzzle fun.

Picture Analogies

Directions: An analogy is a comparison of two things that may be very different, but have something the same about them. For example, let's look at this sentence: "Red is to a strawberry as yellow is to a banana." The first part of that sentence mentions a color (red) and a fruit that is that color (strawberry). The second part mentions a color (yellow) and a fruit that is that color (banana). Complete the analogies by writing the name of the missing things on the blanks.

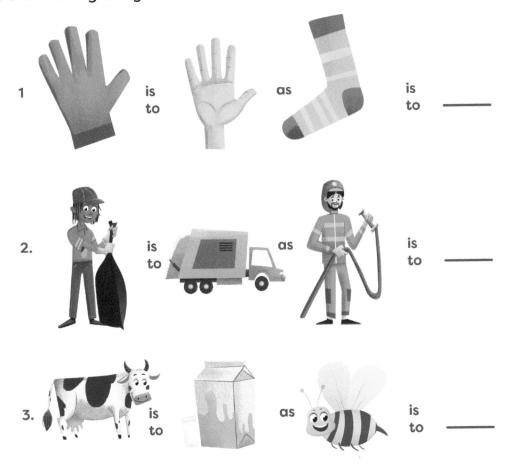

1   is to   as   is to _____

2.   is to   as   is to _____

3.   is to   as   is to _____

Answers on page 132.

PARENT CORNER: Analogies can be tricky, especially for children who haven't been exposed to them before. They require critical thinking to determine the relationship between the items in the analogy. To support your child during this exercise, ask them how the first two items in the analogy are related. Then use that information to figure out the missing object.

Gifted and Talented Workbook for Kids

Directions: This exercise is like the last one, but uses shapes instead of pictures. The shapes in each row are related in some way, but how? Take a look at the first two shapes. How are they related? Then look at the third shape. What shape could you draw to make it related to a fourth shape?

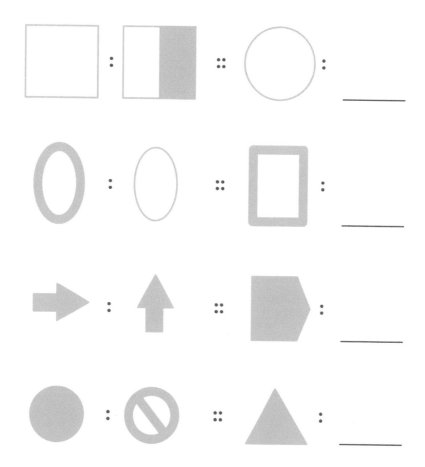

Answers on page 133.

PARENT CORNER: Your child may have a lot of difficulty with this exercise at first, because it's a little more abstract than pictures. In order to help them, focus on one set of shapes at a time. Ask them how the first and second shape are the same, and what makes them different. Then ask them about the third shape: What does it have in common with the first shape? How should they draw the fourth shape?

Word Connection

Directions: Now that you've had some practice with this type of exercise, try these word analogies. Here, you have two sets of words. The first two words are related in the same way the second two words are related. Take a close look at the first set of things in each analogy. Use that relationship to figure out the missing word in each analogy. The first one has been done for you!

Caterpillar	**is to**	Butterfly	**as**	Tadpole	**is to**	Frog
Fish	**is to**	Swim	**as**	Snake	**is to**	_____
Summer	**is to**	Flip Flops	**as**	Winter	**is to**	_____
Apple	**is to**	Tree	**as**	Carrot	**is to**	_____

Answers on page 133.

PARENT CORNER: Word analogies challenge your child to use their higher-order thinking skills and challenge their verbal reasoning abilities. If your child has already completed the previous two exercises, they may fly right through this one. If they're having a hard time, encourage them to figure out the relationship between the first two items in each analogy.

Shape Sleuth

Directions: Your classmate has put different shapes together in groups of three. The shapes in each group have something in common. Look at the groups of shapes, one at a time, and write down what you think they have in common.

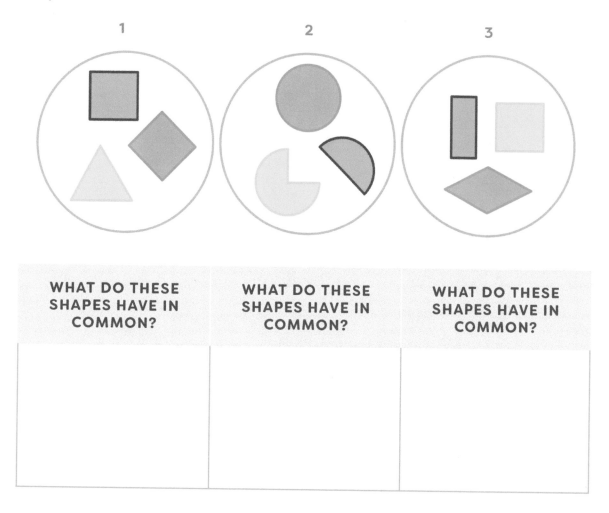

WHAT DO THESE SHAPES HAVE IN COMMON?	WHAT DO THESE SHAPES HAVE IN COMMON?	WHAT DO THESE SHAPES HAVE IN COMMON?

Answers on page 133.

PARENT CORNER: This exercise develops your child's critical thinking skills as they work to decode the reason someone grouped the shapes the way that they did. Your child will need to analyze the shapes in each group to determine their common attribute. If your child has trouble, make sure they focus on only one group at a time. Guide them to describe each shape in the group.

Sort It Out

Directions: You will need a blue and purple crayon for this exercise. Take a look at the 10 shapes shown here. What do they have in common and what is different about them? Put these shapes into four groups and make sure that each group has something in common. Draw the groups in the boxes. You can use the same shape in more than one group as long as it has something in common with the other shapes in the box.

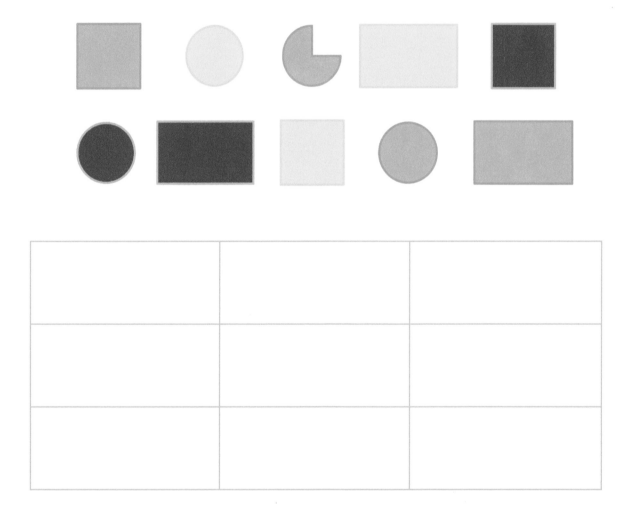

PARENT CORNER: There are many different ways your child can group the shapes, so there is no one correct answer. If your child is stuck and doesn't know where to start, ask them to tell you what the shapes have in common—and what is different about them. When your child is finished, ask them to explain how they decided to group the shapes the way they did.

Which Doesn't Belong?

Directions: It's time to use your detective skills again! All of the objects in each of these four rows have something in common—except for one of them. Identify which object doesn't belong in each row, then draw an X over it to cross it out.

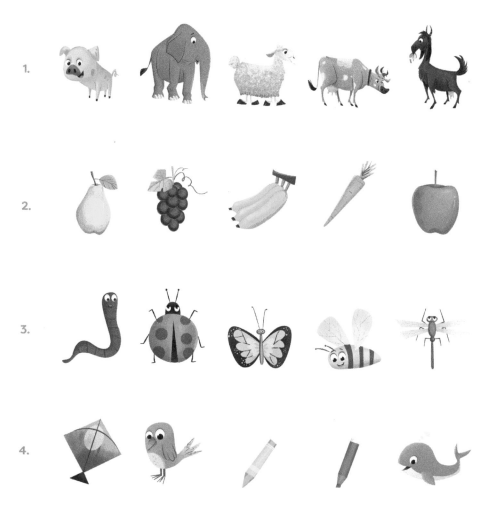

Answers on page 134.

PARENT CORNER: This activity requires your child to make various thought connections to determine the relationships of objects so they can figure out which doesn't belong. They will need to use both reasoning and critical thinking skills to come up with the answers. As your child is working, ask them how they are determining which object doesn't belong in each row.

Add One More

Directions: This exercise is part thinking, part drawing! Each row has three objects that have something in common. Figure out what they have in common, and then draw a fourth object on the line that has the same thing in common.

1.

2.

3.

4.

Answers on page 134.

PARENT CORNER: This exercise builds on the previous one. Rather than asking your child to identify which object doesn't belong, this exercise challenges them to think of a new object that does belong with the others. They still use their reasoning skills to determine the relationships between the objects. They will also need to use higher-order thinking to come up with a brand-new object on their own.

Across and Down

Directions: Each row and column contains three shapes that follow the same pattern. Using the information you get from pattern rows one and two, what should go in the last box? Draw the correct shape in that box to complete the pattern. Do you need a blue crayon to complete it?

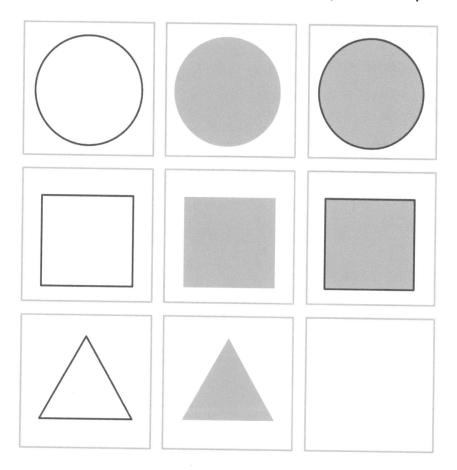

Answers on page 135.

PARENT CORNER: Pattern matrices contain a variety of different shapes in which each row and column in the matrix all follow the same pattern. If your child has completed the sudoku puzzles earlier in this chapter, they may make the connection that this matrix resembles them, since they both use a 3 x 3 table. If they make this observation, praise them for making the connection. However, it's important to clarify to them that this pattern matrix doesn't follow the same rules or directions as a sudoku puzzle.

Cause and Effect

Directions: If you go out in the rain, you will get wet! This is called cause and effect. The rain *causes* you to get wet. Getting wet is the *effect* the rain had on you. The table lists some causes and effects. The first one is done for you. The next three rows show you either a cause or an effect. It's up to you to figure out the cause or effect that's missing.

CAUSE	EFFECT
A child is slowly eating an ice-cream cone in the sun on a hot day.	The ice cream melts.
	Zack has three cavities.
Krista forgot her lunch at home.	
	The plant dies.

Answers on page 135.

PARENT CORNER: Identifying cause-and-effect relationships are a great way to get kids thinking about how and why things happen—and the consequences of certain actions. By providing just the cause, or just the effect, your child will have to use inference and knowledge from their own experiences to determine the missing piece.

CHAPTER 3

Math

This chapter is going to help you sharpen your math skills. It has a collection of fun exercises that will challenge you with number patterns, shapes and figures, and other basic math problems. With so many different activities, you can complete this chapter in order, or pick the exercises that look most interesting to you. Let's do some math!

Adding Shapes

Directions: Let's start with some simple addition problems. The shapes here stand for numbers. For example, in the first problem, you are adding hearts. Three hearts plus two hearts equals five hearts (3 + 2 = 5). In the second problem, four hearts plus a mystery amount makes six hearts in all. What is the amount needed? Draw that number of hearts in the blank space. When you finish the third problem, you can then create your own.

Answers on page 136.

PARENT CORNER: This exercise is a great foundation for the following one. It introduces students to the concept of using problem-solving skills to fill in the blanks of an addition equation. By using pictures and shapes in the equations, your child should be able to better visualize and determine the missing numbers or missing shapes in each one.

Gifted and Talented Workbook for Kids

Addition Detective

Directions: We need an addition detective, and we heard you might be just the right person to call. Use your math skills to figure out the missing numbers in the addition equations. Write the missing numbers on the blanks to make each addition problem correct.

$$5 + \underline{\quad} = 8$$

$$\underline{\quad} + 6 = 9$$

$$4 + \underline{\quad} = 6$$

$$\underline{\quad} + 10 = 10$$

$$7 + \underline{\quad} = 9$$

$$\underline{\quad} + 2 = 5$$

$$1 + \underline{\quad} = 7$$

Answers on page 136.

PARENT CORNER: This exercise is a great way to challenge your child's number sense and understanding of addition and subtraction. It will also develop their understanding of the relationship between the two. If not, they'll likely use a "counting on" strategy where they will count on their fingers to get the sum. If your child is having trouble, encourage them to use their fingers to count, or draw pictures to help them figure it out.

Subtraction Situation

Directions: Oh no! The subtraction problems are each missing a number. Use your math skills to determine what numbers need to go in the blanks to complete each subtraction equation correctly.

$$\_\_\_ - 2 = 8$$

$$\_\_ - 10 = 0$$

$$6 - \_\_\_ = 2$$

$$\_\_\_ - 5 = 4$$

$$5 - \_\_\_ = 3$$

$$10 - \_\_ = 9$$

$$\_\_\_ - 3 = 7$$

Answers on page 136.

PARENT CORNER: As with the previous exercise, this activity will strengthen your child's understanding of addition and subtraction. Although these are subtraction problems, your child may actually use addition skills to determine the missing number in each equation. Remind them that they can use their fingers to count, or draw pictures to help come up with the answers.

More and Less

Directions: Your math detective work continues! Each of the puzzles has numbers missing. To complete the puzzles, look at the instructions on each square and fill in that missing number. For example, in puzzle 1, figure out what number is 10 less than 25, and so on. Puzzles 3 and 4 are different. You need to use the numbers and information in the four boxes to figure out the missing number in the middle.

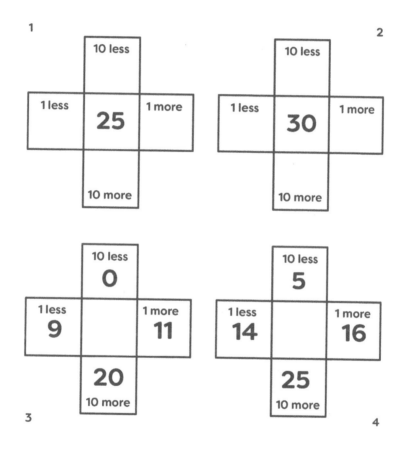

Answers on page 136.

PARENT CORNER: These puzzles will require your child to use their already-practiced addition and subtraction skills to figure out the answers. The top two puzzles are pretty straightforward, and only require some simple addition and subtraction. The bottom two puzzles are a little more complicated. They require some critical thinking for your child to determine the missing number in the middle.

Puppy, Please!

Directions: Melissa really wants a puppy. She saved enough money to buy a leash, a collar, a dog bed, and puppy food. She only has one item left to buy—a tag for the dog's collar, and it's 95 cents. Melissa emptied her piggy bank and needs your help to figure out if she has enough money for the tag. Does she have enough money? Explain your answer.

Answer on page 137.

_____

_____

_____

PARENT CORNER: This powerful exercise combines many math skills into one—including addition, money sense, and comparison (greater than/less than), wrapped into a basic word problem. It's a great way for your child to practice their problem-solving skills, along with a handful of math skills, in a fun and engaging way.

Blooming Math Flowers

Directions: These beautiful blooming math flowers have numbers in their centers and on some of their petals. Help the flowers bloom by figuring out what's missing. The numbers on all the petals must add up to the number in the center of the flower. However, there is a catch—you can't repeat numbers.

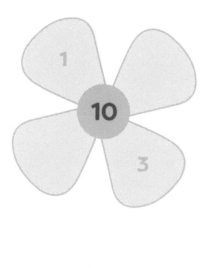

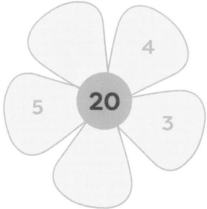

Answers on page 137.

PARENT CORNER: The fact that numbers cannot be repeated is what makes this exercise more challenging. If your child flies through this activity, challenge them further by asking what other numbers they could have put on the blank petals of the flower with the 20 in the middle. There are two possible answers, so see if they can figure out both options.

Three Squares

Directions: In the puzzle here, each square has one circle on either side of it. If you add the numbers in those two circles, you get the number that belongs in the square. Use this rule to figure out what numbers belong in the two empty squares.

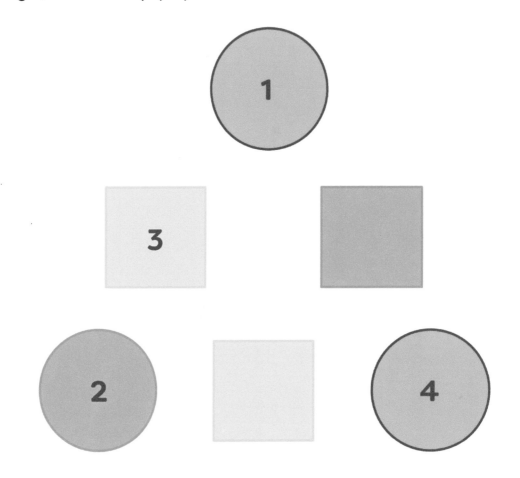

Answers on page 137.

PARENT CORNER: While it uses basic addition, this triangle puzzle presents math in a way that will challenge your child. The concept of this puzzle may be a little tricky to visualize at first, but with a little time, or a little support from you, your child should be able to understand it!

Pyramid Puzzle

Directions: You will need your addition skills to solve these puzzles. Start with the bottom row of the pyramid. The numbers in two boxes next to each other add up to the number above those boxes. For example, in the first pyramid, 5 + 4 = 9, which is why 9 is written in the box above the 5 and the 4. Follow that addition pattern to complete the pyramid.

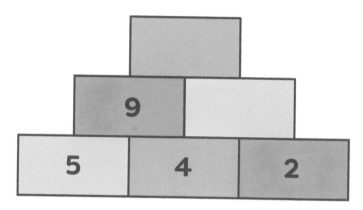

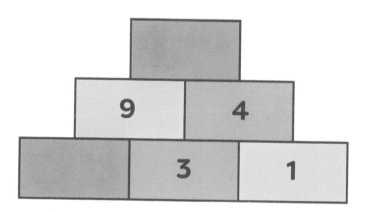

Answers on page 137.

PARENT CORNER: This second pyramid is a little trickier. The directions should give your child all the tools they need to be successful. If they are stuck, help them read through and understand the directions for how the puzzle works.

Completing Carla's Patterns

Directions: Carla started writing some number patterns, but she needs your help to fill in the blanks. To help Carla, you need to figure out the number pattern first. You need to do something to each number to come up with the number after it. The first three numbers will give you that clue. Use the pattern you learned to fill in the blanks.

1, 2, 3, ___, ___, ___

5, 10, 15, ___, ___, ___

2, 4, 6, ___, ___, ___

6, 8, 10, ___, ___, ___

8, 11, 14, ___, ___, ___

Answers on page 138.

PARENT CORNER: This exercise is a great introduction to number patterns, and it will give your child the skills and confidence needed to be successful on the next exercise, which is slightly more difficult. Some of these patterns will introduce your child to a concept called "skip counting," which is basically counting by a certain number (like counting by twos). It is especially helpful when learning multiplication and memorizing multiplication facts.

Martin's Missing Numbers

Directions: Martin thought Carla's math puzzle was fun, so he came up with his own! Look at the numbers that are next to each other and try to figure out what needs to be added to make the number that comes after it. Use that information to figure out the numbers that go in each missing piece of the pattern.

1, 3, 5, _____, 9 _____

3, 6, _____, 12, _____

10, 12, _____, 16, _____

0, 5, _____, _____, 20, 25

4, _____, 12, 16, _____, _____

Answers on page 138.

PARENT CORNER: This activity is more difficult than the ones on the previous page, but they work the same way. This activity reinforces the "skip counting" skill introduced in the previous activity. Your child likely hasn't learned the concept of skip counting yet, but this exercise will build a good foundation for when they do encounter this concept in school.

Dominic's Dominoes

Directions: Dominic used his dominoes to make a pattern. Dominoes are rectangular tiles with one to six dots on one half, and one to six dots on the other. For example, the first domino that Dominic placed has one dot on one half, and six dots on the other. The next one has two dots, and five dots. See if you can figure out Dominic's pattern, and then fill in the blank domino with the correct number of dots on each side.

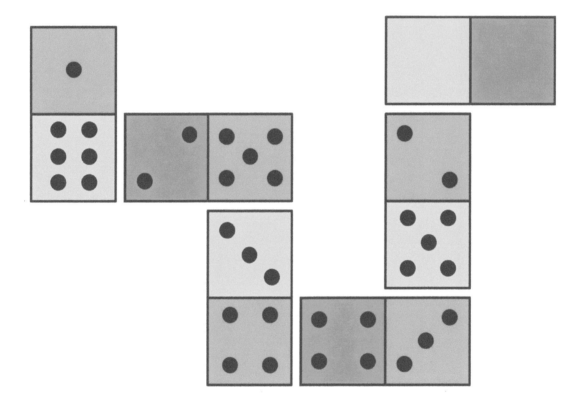

Answer on page 138.

PARENT CORNER: If your child is having trouble identifying the missing domino, encourage them use the skills they learned in previous number pattern puzzles to figure out the pattern that Dominic created. Then they can look at the second-to-last domino and apply the pattern to fill in the final domino.

Let's Measure!

Directions: Today, you are going to practice measuring things! Grab a book and use it to measure some objects around the house. Write the objects you measured and their "book lengths" in the table. Next, pick a book that's a different size. Use it to measure the same objects you did before. Then answer the questions in the table.

OBJECT	# OF BOOK LENGTHS: BOOK ONE	# OF BOOK LENGTHS: BOOK TWO

Does each object have the same book length for book one and two?

Why do you think this is?

What was the longest object?

What was the shortest object?

PARENT CORNER: By measuring things with two different books, your child will begin to develop the concept of units of measure. Although they won't know the official academic terms and different units of measurement, this exercise supports them in constructing their own understanding of the concept.

Get Graphing!

Directions: Graphs are used keep track of things. You can make a graph to show how many toys you have or how many times you ate your favorite foods this week. In this exercise, pick three things you want to graph. Write or draw those things at the bottom of the graph—one thing under each column. Then count how many of those things you have, and color in the bar graph by that same number. Don't forget to give your graph a creative title, too!

PARENT CORNER: By incorporating choice, this graphing exercise is a fun and engaging way to practice graphing. Encouraging your child to graph personal items, such as their own stuffed animals or toys, adds another element of engagement. By having your child create an appropriate title for their graph, they will need to use higher-order thinking skills, ensuring they have a strong understanding of the purpose of that graph element.

Gifted and Talented Workbook for Kids

Shape Search

Directions: The objects we see inside our houses and outside in nature are often geometric shapes. The plates you eat on, for example, are probably circles. Take a close look at the picture and see if you can find all the shapes. Below the picture, write down how many of each shape you found!

Do you see any other shapes? If so, draw them. You can also write the names of them if you know what they're called!

Answers on page 139.

PARENT CORNER: This exercise will engage your child in close observation, and is a great prerequisite to the following exercise. By first identifying geometric shapes in an image, they may be better equipped to find similar shapes in the rooms they're in and the world around them.

Geometry All Around Me

Directions: Geometrical shapes can be found in any room in your house. For example, doors are rectangles. So are most computer screens. In the box, draw the objects you see in your house. Write the name of the shape below each one.

Butterfly Wings

Directions: Butterflies are beautiful. They often have brightly colored wings with pretty patterns. Their wings are identical to each other. This means their left wings look the same as their right wings! That's called symmetry. The butterflies are divided into two separate halves. Draw a line to match the two halves that are symmetrical. Pay close attention to the shapes and colors that each wing has.

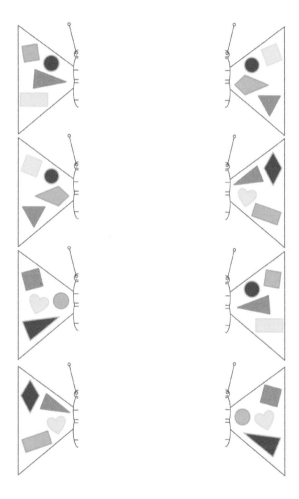

Answers on page 139.

PARENT CORNER: This exercise combines two math concepts—geometry and symmetry—in a fun and engaging way. Your child will need to use their observations to compare and contrast in order to find the correct match for the butterfly wings. If they need help, cover all the halves except the one they are working on. Have them focus on one of the choices at a time to see if there is a match.

A New Look for a Ladybug!

Directions: Ladybugs are also symmetrical creatures. Usually, ladybugs have round black spots on them, but this is your chance to get creative and design a new look for the ladybug! Use geometrical shapes, like squares, triangles, and circles, to decorate the ladybug's wings. You can also use colored pencils or crayons to add color, too. Just make sure that the two wings are symmetrical!

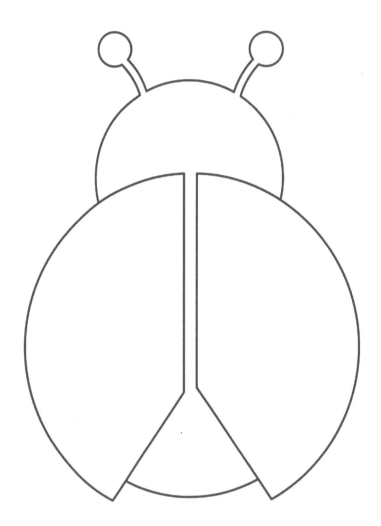

PARENT CORNER: This exercise uses the same concepts of geometry and symmetry, but at a higher level of thinking. After completing the previous activity, your child should have a good understanding of the concept and should be able to succeed here with minimal to no support.

Gifted and Talented Workbook for Kids

Piece of Cake

Directions: It's your birthday and it's time to eat cake! Your mom made two cakes that are exactly the same size. The only difference is that one is cut into eight equal slices, and the other is cut into four equal slices. You have a choice:

★ You can have two slices of the cake that is cut into eight pieces.

★ You can have one slice of the cake that's cut into four pieces.

You can use the picture to help you decide!

Which option would you choose? Does it matter? Explain why you made your choice.

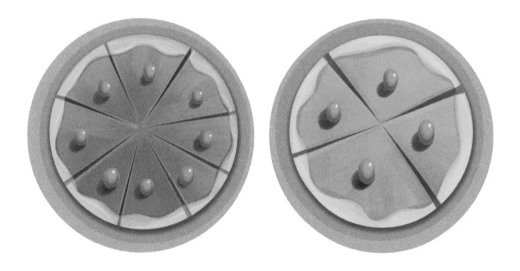

Answer on page 140.

PARENT CORNER: It's likely that your child has not had direct instruction on fractions before—so this exercise may be tricky for them. They likely won't know the words *fractions* or *equivalent*, but they should understand and be able to use words like *pieces* and *equal* or phrases such as "the same size" to explain their reasoning on this exercise.

Tricky Triangle Challenge

Directions: Look at the picture. What do you see? Triangles, right? But how many are there? Look very closely and count them. You can use a pencil or some colored pencils to help outline the triangles you see as you count. This one is definitely tricky, so take your time.

Number of tangled triangles is _____.

Answer on page 140.

PARENT CORNER: At first glance, your child may not see all of the triangles hidden in this puzzle. Some are obvious, while others take a little focus to notice. Encourage them to take a closer look to find all of the triangles in the puzzle. Using crayons or colored pencils to outline the individual triangles as they find them will help.

How Many on the Bus?

Directions: Are you ready to solve a riddle? Read this riddle closely. You need to figure out how many kids are left on the bus at the end!

This morning, the bus driver picked up 5 kids at the bus stop. At the next stop, 3 more kids got on the bus. Next, the bus dropped off 2 kids at their school. The bus went to one more bus stop and picked up 1 more kid. Finally, the bus dropped off 7 kids at their school. How many kids are left on the bus?

If you are stuck, try drawing a picture in the space to help you keep track of the kids who are getting on and off the bus!

The total number of kids that are still on the bus is _____.

Answer on page 140.

PARENT CORNER: This riddle has many parts, so it may be tricky or overwhelming for your child. Encourage them to take it one piece at a time. If they haven't tried it already, you might suggest that they draw a picture to help them visualize and track the students getting on and off the bus.

PART 2

Fun Activities and Projects

This section is full of activities and projects you can do at home that will stretch your creativity and feed your curiosity. There is something for everyone: art projects, science experiments, ways to explore nature, and more. Some of the activities in this section are great for you to do on your own. Others are fun to do with your family so you can explore, learn, and create together!

CHAPTER 4

Let's Be Creative!

The activities in this chapter include art projects, story-telling, games, and music. Some of them you'll do right on the pages of this book. For others, you'll need some things from around the house, such as simple art supplies like paint, beads, pipe cleaners, and chalk. Each activity has a list of things you'll need, so read through before you begin. Have fun and be inspired!

What Can It Be?

Description: If you need help, try turning this book sideways or upside down and complete your drawing that way. Look at objects or things around you for ideas.

MATERIALS:

Pencil, colored pencils, markers, or crayons

Optional: extra paper for additional drawings

INSTRUCTIONS:

1. Look at the shapes in the box. What do you see?

2. Think of ways to use the lines and shapes together to create one drawing, instead of one drawing for each line or shape.

3. Once you have your idea, use your pencils or crayons to make your drawing. If you have a couple of different ideas, you can use another piece of paper to make more art!

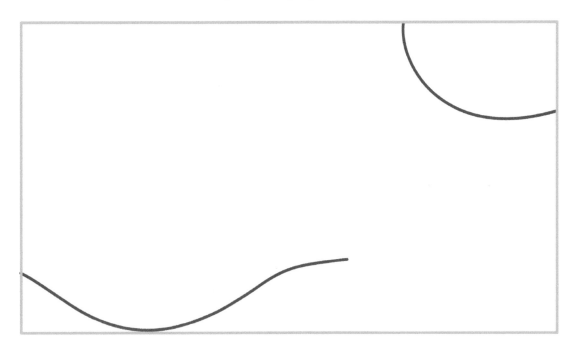

PARENT CORNER: This activity is great for getting your child to think beyond the obvious, promoting out-of-the-box thinking. If your child enjoys this activity and wants to do more, simply draw one or two shapes and/or squiggles on a piece of paper and encourage them turn those into a picture!

What Else Am I?

||||||||||||||||||||||||||||||||||||||||||||||||||||||||||||||||||||||||||||||||||||||||||||||||

Description: For this activity, try not to draw the first thing you think of. Draw something unexpected. In other words, think about what else this picture could become.

MATERIALS:

Pencil, colored pencils, markers, or crayons

INSTRUCTIONS:

1. Take a look at the picture. What does it look like? It probably looks a lot like a butterfly's wing to you.

2. Take time to think about what else it could be.

3. Draw your new idea.

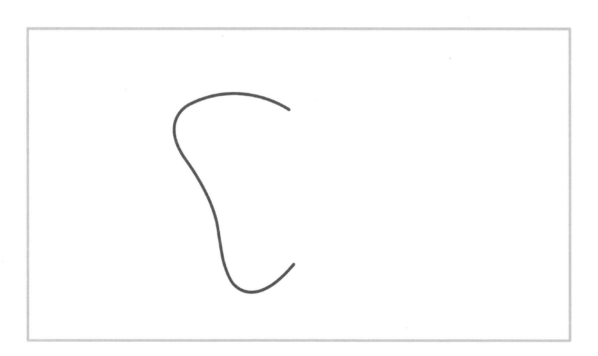

PARENT CORNER: If your child is having trouble trying to figure out what else the shape could be, encourage them to turn the book around and look at it from a different angle.

Super Scribbles

Description: Clouds are cool. Maybe you've seen a big fluffy cloud that looked like a bunny or a face! In this activity, you are going to do something similar. Instead of looking at clouds, scribble on the paper and see if you can find any pictures hidden in them!

MATERIALS:

A pencil

Colored pencils, markers, or crayons

INSTRUCTIONS:

1. Using a pencil, scribble in the empty box. Just let your hand go wherever it wants to within the box.

2. Take a good look at what you've drawn. Can you find any pictures in your scribble?

3. Use colored pencils, markers, or crayons to color in and add details to the pictures you found!

4. If you're having trouble seeing any pictures or objects in your scribbles, turn the workbook around and look at them from a different angle.

PARENT CORNER: This activity makes your child use their imagination and critical thinking to identify pictures within their own scribbles. If your child has never looked for shapes in the clouds, it might be a good idea to do that before completing this activity. This will help them learn the concept of finding pictures in other things.

Making Music

Description: Using things you can find around the house, today is about making your own unique instrument. It can be like instruments you've seen before, or it can be something totally new! Once you've invented your instrument, play it. Before you begin, make sure your parents are okay with you using the things you find.

MATERIALS:

Things from around the house that can be used to make an instrument (pots, pans, tissue boxes, and rubber bands are some good ideas)

INSTRUCTIONS:

1. Look around the house for things to use for your instrument.

2. Use the materials to put your instrument together, just the way you want it.

3. Give your instrument a creative name!

4. Play your instrument, and see how it sounds. Try playing a new song, or try playing a song you already know.

PARENT CORNER: Since this activity is open-ended, rather than having step-by-step instructions on how to create a specific instrument, your child has the opportunity to be really creative here. If they've come up with a made-up instrument, ask your child what they would call it and have them explain why. Think of this as a two-in-one activity. They will use creativity to make their instrument, and then create a song or beat they can play on their instrument.

Telling Toy Tales

Description: Do you have a favorite toy? Who do you think invented it? In this activity, you're going to think like an inventor. Your goal is to figure out what the inventor is like and why they invented something—in this case, your toy. Pick your favorite toy, and then imagine who created it!

MATERIALS:

Your favorite toy

Your imagination

INSTRUCTIONS:

1. Place your favorite toy in front of you. Take a good look at it. Pick it up, turn it upside down. Think about its color, texture. What do you do with the toy?

2. Think about the person who may have invented your favorite toy. Why do you think they invented that toy? If it's a stuffed animal, is it supposed to tossed around like a ball?

3. Make up a story about the person that invented the toy and why they invented it.

4. Tell your story to someone!

PARENT CORNER: This activity will get your child thinking about things from another person's perspective. It requires them to make inferences based on things they know. Your child will engage in higher-level thinking, while also having fun using their creativity and imagination! This activity also connects well to some of the language arts exercises found in chapter 1 of this workbook.

When I Grow Up

Description: There are so many things you can be or do when you grow up. You may choose to do the same thing someone in your family does. Maybe you want to be a teacher like your dad or a doctor like your mom. Maybe you will decide to become something totally different.

MATERIALS:

Paper

Pencil, crayons, colored pencils, and/or markers

INSTRUCTIONS:

1. Think about things you like to do and things you like to learn about. For example, maybe you like reading, solving math problems, exploring nature, or maybe even singing or making music.

2. Now that you know what you like to do, think of different jobs that use the skills that you like to do. Ask an adult to help you if you can't think of anything right away.

3. Draw a picture on the paper of yourself doing a job you want to do. For example, if you want to be a firefighter, you could draw yourself in a firefighter outfit, or you could draw a picture of yourself putting out a fire with a big hose!

4. Tell a family member or friend a story about how you will become that person.

PARENT CORNER: This activity has so many benefits. It helps your child think introspectively, gets them thinking about their future, and requires them to really consider the steps they need to take to reach their goals. When they tell a story about how they will become that person, it helps them envision what they need to do to achieve their dream.

Guess What I Am!

Description: You'll need a group of people for this game, because it involves two teams. The object is for one person on a team to act out a word, while their teammates guess what it is. The team with the most correct guesses wins. Grab some paper, a pencil, and get guessing!

MATERIALS:

People (ideally an even number, but if there is an odd number, one person can be the time-keeper or one team can have an extra person)

Small strips of paper (10 to 20 strips)

Pencil or pen

Something to hold the strips of paper (a hat, bowl, or small bag works well)

Timer

INSTRUCTIONS:

1. On each piece of paper, write an object, action, or something that you will act out.

2. Fold up all the strips of paper and put them in a hat or bowl.

3. Split the players into two teams with at least two people per team.

4. One person on team 1 picks a strip of paper, reads it, and keeps what's written on that paper a secret.

5. Set the timer for 30 seconds and start it.

6. The person acts out what is on their paper. While they're acting, everyone else on their team should shout out guesses for what the object is.

7. Once someone gets the answer correct or the time runs out, that turn is over. Put the paper aside so it won't be used again.

8. Repeat steps 4 to 6 with a person from team 2.

9. Teams alternate turns until everyone has had a chance to act or until the strips of paper run out.

PARENT CORNER: This activity requires creativity and even exercises your child's critical thinking as they decide what to write on the strips of paper. To keep this game light, you can skip the timer and just play for fun.

Gifted and Talented Workbook for Kids

Reimagine and Repurpose

Description: Inventors are often unique thinkers. They see a problem and come up with a new way to solve it. Today, you are going to come up with a new use for something you already have. Put on your inventor cap and let's get started!

MATERIALS:

An object to reinvent

Pencil, crayons, colored pencils, and/or markers

INSTRUCTIONS:

1. Find an object inside your house that you think may be able to be used differently than it is used now. This could be a roll of toilet paper, or a spatula from the kitchen, or even a blanket.

2. Think about a way that object could solve another problem.

3. In the box, draw or write about how that object can be used in a new way.

PARENT CORNER: This activity is great for gifted learners who have a knack for inventing, or for taking everyday objects and repurposing them into something new and unique. For some children, this activity may come totally naturally to them. Others might have a bit of a challenge. Either way, it will get your child thinking creatively and will support the development of outside-the-box thinking skills!

Home, Sweet Home

Description: Today, you are going to design a cozy house for your stuffed animals. It can be for one favorite stuffed animal or action figure. If you feel inspired, you can even make a few different houses for your stuffed pals! To prepare, save empty tissue boxes or ask a parent to keep the box next time they get a package. In the meantime, think about the house you want to create.

MATERIALS:

1 or more stuffed animals

Small to medium cardboard boxes

Markers

Optional: things to decorate with, such as ribbon, colored paper, or other materials that can be used or repurposed for this activity

INSTRUCTIONS:

1. Pick a stuffed animal that you think would like a new home.

2. Find a cardboard box that they will fit inside with room to spare.

3. Think about the types of things your stuffed animal would want in their house. What decorations would they like? Do they have a favorite color?

4. Use your imagination, art supplies, and any other materials to turn the cardboard box into the perfect home for your stuffed animal. Remember that you can use more than one box to give your house more than one room.

PARENT CORNER: This activity engages your child to reimagine how they can turn a cardboard box into a cozy home for their stuffed animal. It also helps them consider other perspectives and preferences. They need to put themselves in their stuffed animal's shoes to design a space that is perfect for them.

Art from Nature

Description: There is beauty in nature, and there is beauty in art. You are going to use those two things—art and nature—and put them together to create something beautiful. Go outside and use nature to inspire your inner artist!

MATERIALS:

Items from nature, such as leaves, flowers, or sticks (optional)

Colored pencils, markers, crayons, and/or paint and a paintbrush

Paper

Glue (optional)

INSTRUCTIONS:

1. Go outside and look for pretty things all around you. Let the colors, sounds, shapes, and feelings of nature inspire you as an artist.

2. If you'd like, collect items from nature such as leaves, flowers, or sticks to use in your art.*

3. Use your supplies to create a piece of art that also shows the beauty of nature.

4. If you collected items from nature, think about ways to include these objects in your artwork. You can paint some rocks or flowers, or glue different sticks to paper.

Caution: Always check with an adult before picking up leaves and flowers. Some plants have thorns or are poisonous.

PARENT CORNER: A lot of times, if a child has just a blank canvas, they don't know where to start. By bringing your child outside to find inspiration, you are helping them find a starting point for their art.

Picture This

Description: This activity will help you really picture yourself doing super cool things. Using chalk and some props, you will create a scene and then become part of it. When you are finished, a parent can take a photo so you can see how cool you look! This activity might be a little hard to imagine at first, but once you get started, your creativity will flow.

MATERIALS:

Sidewalk chalk

Optional: some props to add to the chalk art, as needed (for example, a real basketball to go with a chalk-drawn basketball hoop or goggles to go with a chalk underwater scene)

Camera or phone (to take a photo)

INSTRUCTIONS:

1. Think about a place you really want to go to, or something you want to do. Maybe you'd like to snorkel with fish in a coral reef. If you are a sports fan, maybe you'd like to play with your favorite athlete.

2. Once you have narrowed down your idea, go outside to begin your drawing.

3. Using chalk, draw a giant scene for the place or activity you chose. You will need to fit into the scene, so keep that in mind when you are drawing.

4. When you're finished with the drawing, think if you need any props for the picture. For example, grab a real basketball if you drew a basketball hoop—maybe put on a basketball jersey.

5. Lie down on the ground and pose so you look like you are really in your chalk scene.

6. Have an adult take a picture of you from above.

7. Try different poses until you find one you like. The more active the pose, the better!

PARENT CORNER: This activity might be a little hard for your child to visualize, since they need to think about multiple perspectives. They must visualize how the chalk scene looks on the sidewalk. They also have to consider how to pose so it looks like they are in the scene when viewed from above. Let your child take charge if they can. If they have trouble, feel free to help by giving them ideas or suggestions on what they can draw or what type of scene they might like to create. Once they successfully make one chalk scene and see how it turns out in a picture, they will likely gain a full under-standing of this activity and be inspired to create even more.

Leaf Stamps

Description: Leaves are awesome. Not only do they look pretty on trees, but once they fall on the ground, they can be used for cool art projects. For this project, you're going to go outside and collect at least five leaves. Be sure to look carefully for the most interesting shapes and textures.

MATERIALS:

Leaves collected from outside*

Washable tempera paint in several colors (choose brown, orange, and red to create fall-colored leaves, or shades of green to create spring/summer leaves)

A large paintbrush

White paper or construction paper

INSTRUCTIONS:

1. Lay your leaves out on the table.

2. Take a leaf and paint one side of it with your paintbrush.

3. Carefully flip over the leaf and press the painted side onto your paper.

4. Gently lift the leaf up to see your leaf print.

5. Repeat these steps with as many leaves as you like until your painting is just how you want it.

Caution: Always check with an adult before picking up leaves. Some plants have thorns or are poisonous.

PARENT CORNER: By using leaves as stamps, your child will not only use their creativity and artistic skills, but they will also make observations about their leaves. If your child finds something else in nature that they want to use as a stamp, let them try it. It's great to let them explore and make discoveries and observations based on their hands-on experiences!

Mapping My Neighborhood

Description: This activity is about getting to know your neighborhood. First, you'll go for a walk around your neighborhood. Then you'll draw a map. If you're feeling extra creative, you can redesign your neighborhood to make it a more crazy, wild, or imaginative place!

MATERIALS:

Pencil

Blank paper

INSTRUCTIONS:

1. With an adult, take a walk around your neighborhood. Go slowly and take a close look at everything around you. What do you notice? Are there lots of trees? Other houses? Do you see any animals?

2. Once you have a good idea of what your neighborhood looks like, go home and draw your map.

3. Make sure you include streets, driveways, trees, other houses, and any other details that you think are important.

4. If you know the name of a street, or know who lives in a certain house, label those on the map to make it even more detailed.

5. Once you've drawn your map, think about things you'd like to change. Redesign your neighborhood on another piece of paper using your imagination. You can include things that are realistic, or you can let your imagination run wild!

PARENT CORNER: Paying attention to small details in the world around them helps your child gain a broader but more detailed view of the world. By offering the option to redesign the neighborhood, your child can truly let their imagination run wild!

Stargazer

Description: Take a minute to look up at the night sky. What did you see? You probably saw lots of stars. Look closer and you may see some pictures in those groups of stars—a crab, a bull, or a lion are a few. Those images are called constellations. Today, you get to design your very own constellation!

MATERIALS:

Pencil

INSTRUCTIONS:

1. When it is dark, go outside and take a look at the sky. This is best to do when the moon isn't out.

2. Look closely at the stars. What do you notice? Do you see any patterns? Do any of them make a picture?

3. In the box on the next page, draw a group of stars you saw. Use small dots to represent stars.

4. Try to connect some or all of the dots to create a picture.

5. You've just created a new constellation! Give the constellation a name and write it on the line on the next page.

My Dream Bedroom

Description: Think for a minute about creating your dream bedroom. What would that look like? What color would you paint the walls? What type of furniture would you have? Have you dreamed of a slide or rock climbing wall? Maybe cool bunk beds? For this activity, you get to imagine and draw exactly how you want your dream bedroom.

MATERIALS:

Pencil, colored pencils, crayons, and/or markers

Blank paper or graph paper

Optional: ruler

INSTRUCTIONS:

1. Draw the outline of your room on a piece of paper. If your room is a rectangle, for example, draw a rectangle on the paper. If straight lines are important to you, use a ruler.

2. Continue to think about how you want your room to be arranged.

3. Draw the furniture, toys, and anything else you can think of.

4. Finally, give your room some color to add even more excitement to your room!

PARENT CORNER: This activity gives your child the opportunity to step into a designing role and let their wildest imagination come out. With no limits or boundaries, it's really fun to see what kids come up with. Maybe it will inspire career choices later in life!

Beautiful Beaded Bracelet

Description: You learned about patterns earlier in this book. This activity uses patterns to create a beautiful, beaded bracelet that you can wear. Make one for you, your friend, or a family member. They make thoughtful gifts.

MATERIALS:

Colored beads that a pipe cleaner can fit through

Pipe cleaners (1 per bracelet)

Optional: pencil, colored pencils, markers, and/or crayons

INSTRUCTIONS:

1. Decide what colored beads you want to use. Pick at least two colors.

2. Decide on a pattern. It could be something like red-red-blue-red-red-blue or red-blue-red-blue. The possibilities are endless.

3. Lay out the beads on the table to follow the patterns you like best.

4. String the beads onto a pipe cleaner, double checking to make sure that the colors are in the right order for your pattern.

5. When you have enough beads on your pipe cleaner, ask an adult to twist the ends together to create a bracelet that is big enough for you to slide on and off.

PARENT CORNER: This one activity encompasses many skills beyond just creativity. Making a pattern engages math and critical thinking skills. Stringing the beads onto the pipe cleaner develops fine motor skills. Your child should be able to complete all the prior steps on their own, but may need help from you to twist the ends of the pipe cleaner together.

Act It Out

Description: In books, the pictures show what is going on in the story, what the characters look like, and where the story takes place. These details help the reader see the story in their mind. Plays use costumes, objects called props, backdrops, and movement to show all of those same things. In this activity, you'll turn your favorite picture-book story into a play. You can perform on your own or use puppets or dolls as the characters. Another idea is to invite other people to act with you in the play with you.

MATERIALS:

Picture book

2 or 3 people to act in the play

Costumes or outfits that go with characters in the book

Optional: pencil and paper, stuffed animals, dolls, puppets, or other props

INSTRUCTIONS:

1. Grab your favorite storybook, or one that you think would be good to act out as a play.

2. Read the book to figure out who are the main characters.

3. In the table on the next page, write down all of the main characters in your play. Describe what they should wear and what they will say. You could even draw pictures.

4. Practice what you are going to say during the play.

5. Put together the costumes or outfits that the characters will wear.

6. Get an audience together. It can be real people or a group of stuffed animals.

7. Perform your play. Bravo!

Main character's name:	Costume ideas:	What will the character say?
Character 2's name:	Costume ideas:	What will the character say?
Character 3's name:	Costume ideas:	What will the character say?

PARENT CORNER: This activity is perfect for an outgoing child who has a flair for the dramatic, or can help shy and reserved come out of their shell. Allow your child to really take charge of this activity completely on their own. To make it extra special, record the play and send the video to friends or family. Make sure to get your child's permission first.

Singer, Songwriter, Star

Description: Have you always dreamed of being a singer, songwriter, or music star? Here's your chance to try out all of those things! Using the tune of a song you already know, create new lyrics, or words, and then perform your song. You will be the star!

MATERIALS:

Pencil

INSTRUCTIONS:

1. Pick a song that you know well—one that you could sing yourself.

2. Think about what you want the new song to be about. Use that subject to guide your songwriting.

3. Write your new song on the lines.

4. Once your lyrics are complete, you need to practice your song.

5. Sing it all the way through several times, until you have it memorized.

6. Perform your song in front of an audience. This can be friends or family, or a group of your dolls or stuffed animals!

_____

_____

_____

_____

PARENT CORNER: This activity might be out of your child's comfort zone, or it might be right up their alley! If they want to write the song but not perform it, that is completely okay. The main creative element in this activity is the actual songwriting process. The performance is a fun addition, and a great creative outlet for an outgoing child or one who loves to perform.

Make a Menu

Description: If you had a restaurant, what would be on the menu? In this activity, you get to decide! The next time you go to a restaurant, remember to take a close look at the menu. You can also ask your parents to take a picture of it. Then, when you are back home, get out a piece of paper and use it to help you come up with your own menu.

MATERIALS:

Paper

Colored pencils, markers, and/or crayons

INSTRUCTIONS:

1. Think about which meal of the day you want to design a menu for. Will it be for breakfast, brunch, lunch, or dinner? Midnight snack?

2. Next, think about what dishes you want to highlight on your menu. They can be anything you dream of. Maybe you'd like to have strawberry waffles or French fry pizza!

3. Once you've settled on your menu items, begin to write creative names for the dishes your restaurant would serve. Don't forget to include prices.

4. When all of your items are listed, add drawings and color to your menu.

PARENT CORNER: This activity is a great way for your child to get creative while tapping into their own interests and tastes. They might make a really serious menu, or they may choose to design silly, wild, or unique dishes. Depending on how outrageous their dream menu is, you can expand on this activity by making some or all of the dishes with your child. This will give them a sense of ownership and pride, and will make this activity very meaningful to them.

Abstract Art

Description: Abstract art is a kind of art that doesn't use the expected shapes for objects. Usually, it isn't easy to figure out what the artist was trying to paint. A person looking at the art may see just colors and shapes, but the artist knows what that their abstract art represents. Anyone can make abstract art. Let's give it a try!

MATERIALS:

Colored pencils, markers, crayons, watercolor, and/or washable paint

Paintbrushes (if using paint)

Blank paper or a canvas

INSTRUCTIONS:

1. Think about a mood or situation that you feel strongly about. It could be something like "sadness" or "feeling sunshine on your face."

2. Close your eyes and imagine what that mood or situation might look like. What colors do you see? What shapes?

3. Draw or paint different colors, shapes, and patterns to represent the subject you've chosen.

4. When your art is finished, tell a story about it. What feelings does it represent? What deeper meaning could this piece of art have?

PARENT CORNER: Creating abstract art is a great outlet for your child to express their feelings, moods, or ideas in a way that is meaningful. This low-stress type of art is perfect for children with perfectionist tendencies because it forces them to think differently about being creative. To expand on this activity, use the Internet or a local art museum to explore some abstract art with your child.

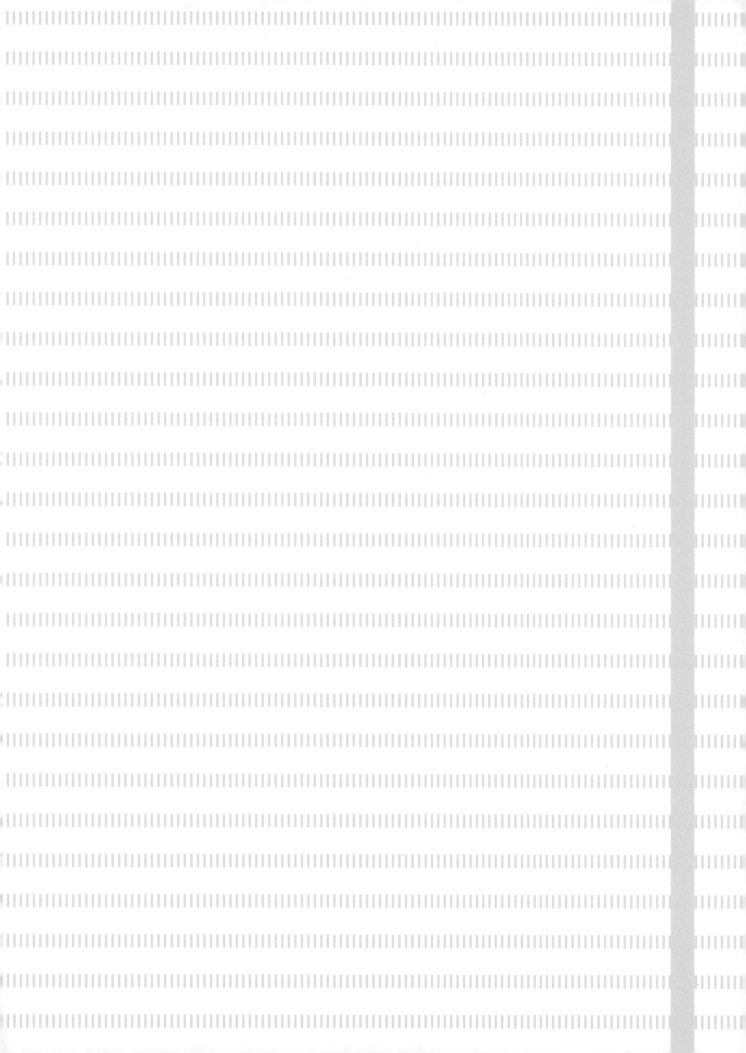

CHAPTER 5

Let's Do Science!

This chapter is full of fun indoor and outdoor science projects to help you learn about the world around you. Maybe you already know that you love science. Perhaps you aren't sure if you think science is fun. These activities are perfect for you, either way. You might even discover a new interest or passion in the process!

Magical Mysterious Moon

Description: Have you ever noticed that the moon's shape is always changing? Sometimes you can see a huge round moon, while other times you just see a small part of it. Over the next few weeks, be an astronomer and study the moon. See if you can identify any patterns.

MATERIALS:

Pencil

Clock

INSTRUCTIONS:

1. When it's dark, go outside and take a look at the moon.

2. Write the date and time in the table on the next page, then draw a picture to show what the moon looks like at that time.

3. Look at the moon at the same time every two or three days. Be sure to track what you see in the table on the next page.

4. Once you've looked at the moon eight different times, study the table and note what the moon looked like each night.

5. Talk with an adult about what you notice. Does the moon look the same or different on different nights? Do you see any patterns? What do you think is happening?

Date:	Date:	Date:	Date:
Time:	Time:	Time:	Time:
Date:	Date:	Date:	Date:
Time:	Time:	Time:	Time:

PARENT CORNER: This inquiry-based exercise gives your child the opportunity to make their own observations of moon phases. By engaging your child's natural curiosity, this activity will encourage them to reflect on their findings, investigate further, and discuss their newfound knowledge with you. If your child is eager to learn more about the moon, or has questions about it that you may not know the answers to, check out Moon.NASA.gov for in-depth information, pictures, answers to commonly asked questions, and so much more all related to our moon.

Up Close

Description: Some things look very different when you see them up close. That's what this activity is all about. You will need a magnifying glass. It is a tool with special glass that lets you see tiny details that you may not have ever noticed. Get ready to be amazed!

MATERIALS:

Objects from nature

Pencil

Magnifying glass

INSTRUCTIONS:

1. Go outside and find some natural objects that interest you, such as sticks, leaves, or even tree bark.*

2. When you're back inside, write down the names of each object that you collected in the table on the next page.

3. Next, draw what the objects look like.

4. Use the magnifying glass to look closely at each of the objects.

5. After you look at each item through the magnifying glass, draw any new details that you see.

6. Tell an adult or friend what you notice about each object. Is there anything you saw through the magnifying glass that you couldn't see before?

Caution: Always check with an adult before picking up leaves. Some plants have thorns or are poisonous.

NAME OF OBJECT	DRAW WHAT IT LOOKS LIKE WITHOUT A MAGNIFYING GLASS	DRAW WHAT IT LOOKS LIKE THROUGH THE MAGNIFYING GLASS

Nature Grouping

Description: Nature is full of objects that have different colors, shapes, textures, or sizes. But many of these objects also have things in common. For example, a leaf and a piece of grass may be different shapes, but have the same smooth texture. Today, you're going to group together natural objects that have something in common. Challenge yourself to make groups based on something more than color.

MATERIALS:

At least 10 objects from nature

INSTRUCTIONS:

1. Go outside and collect 10 natural objects. Rocks, leaves, sticks, and flowers are good choices.*

2. When you're back home, place all of the items you collected on a table.

3. Look at each one separately. Notice each object's shape, color, size, and even how it feels.

4. Look at all of the objects together. What do you notice is the same and what do you notice is different?

5. Place the objects in at least two different groups based on things they have in common, such as texture, shape, or size.

6. Explain to a grown-up why you grouped the objects the way you did.

7. Can you group those same 10 objects in a different way? Explain the new groups to a grown-up.

Caution: Always check with an adult before picking up leaves. Some plants have thorns or are poisonous.

PARENT CORNER: This object classification activity helps your child make connections about nature and the world around them. By exploring natural science this way, your child will become more familiar with the similarities, differences, details, and connections found in nature. Encourage your child to choose categories with details they might not have noticed at first glance.

Litter Less

Description: Litter is trash that is left in places it shouldn't be, such as parks, yards, or on the side of the street. Have you ever noticed litter—like paper or plastic bags? Litter is bad for the environment, and today you're going to make a poster to convince people to litter less.

MATERIALS:

Markers, crayons, and/ or colored pencils

Paper

INSTRUCTIONS:

1. Go outside and look for litter. To avoid germs, don't touch any of the trash. Just look and see what trash you see on the ground.

2. Talk with a grown-up about what you saw.

3. When you get back home, list all of the items you saw outside.

4. Using a piece of paper, create a poster that encourages people to stop littering. Be sure to draw the litter you saw and include a title at the top of your poster.

PARENT CORNER: Littering and pollution are big issues that impact our world. This activity simply introduces your child to littering, and opens their eyes so they can see how big of a problem it really is. There is so much more to learn about this topic. If your child shows interest in learning more, head to your local library and check out some books on the topic.

I Spy . . . Nature!

Description: If you've ever played the game "I Spy," this activity will be familiar to you! For this game, you can only pick items from nature such as trees, plants, animals—or anything else natural that you see around you. This is a fun activity to do while on a nature walk with your family, or even while just walking around the neighborhood.

MATERIALS:

None

INSTRUCTIONS:

1. Go outside with your family or friends, or go on a nature walk if there are trails nearby.

2. Pick an object in nature, but don't tell anyone what you picked.

3. Describe your object in just one or two words. You might say, "I see something tall." Let everyone guess what it might be.

4. Repeat step 3 until someone guesses your object correctly.

5. The person who guessed correctly is the next person to describe an object.

PARENT CORNER: This activity is a great way to encourage mindfulness and observation for everyone involved. Describing what they "spy" in detail encourages your child to analyze and look more closely at things in order to see things they may not have noticed before. When it's their turn to guess an object based on someone else's description, they need to think from that person's perspective.

Exploring Earth's Surface

Description: The surface of our Earth is made up of two types of materials—natural and human-made. Natural materials, also called natural resources, are things such as stones. Human-made materials, or human-made resources, are things that have been created by humans, such as buildings. Let's explore the natural and human-made resources around you, and analyze them to find things that are the same and different about them.

MATERIALS:

None

INSTRUCTIONS:

1. Go outside and notice the different materials, textures, or surfaces you see around you. Look closely and touch them. How many different textures, materials, and surfaces do you see? Which are natural? Which are human-made?

2. Once you've identified surfaces that are natural and those that are human-made, compare them. Do the natural objects have anything in common with each other? Do you notice any big differences? Do the human-made objects have anything in common with each other, or any big differences?

3. Compare the natural and human-made objects. Is anything the same between the two groups? Are there any big differences between them?

4. Talk about what you found with someone.

PARENT CORNER: This activity introduces your child to the concept of natural versus human-made resources—one that they will explore throughout elementary school. By identifying which materials are natural and which are human-made, your child is already applying knowledge of this concept in a meaningful way. By making observations and constructing their own connections and understandings, they are building meaningful knowledge through this inquiry process.

Bird Watcher

Description: Bird-watching is a fun hobby that many people enjoy. It's really interesting to see different types of birds and watch how they interact with each other. The best way to watch birds is to make a bird feeder. This will attract them to your yard.

MATERIALS:

Box cutter or X-Acto knife*

Milk carton, empty and clean (a paper half-gallon carton works best, but you can use other cartons as well)

Hole punch

String

Scissors*

Birdseed

INSTRUCTIONS:

1. Ask an adult to use a box cutter or X-Acto knife to cut out a square opening in one side of the carton. The bottom of the square should be about two inches from the bottom of the carton and the top should be about halfway up the carton, as shown in the picture.

2. Ask an adult to punch a hole in the top of the milk carton. If the carton has a cap in the way, punch a hole on either side of it.

3. Ask an adult to cut a 10-inch-long piece of string. Put the string through the hole in the top of the carton. You will use it to hang your feeder.

4. Put some birdseed in the bottom of the carton. Make sure there is a thick layer of seed, but not so much that it spills over the edge.

5. With an adult's help, find a tree branch or other place to hang your bird feeder. Try to put it in a place where you can see it from a window, so you can easily watch from inside the house and won't scare birds away.

Caution: An adult should handle the knife and scissors and do all the cutting for this project.

6. Over the next few days, watch the birds that come to your feeder. What do they look like? How do they interact with each other? Do any other animals come to the feeder? If so, what happens?

7. Refill your bird feeder as often as you want to keep the birds coming!

Wild for Wildflowers!

Description: Wildflowers grow and blossom in nature. If you live some-place that is warm year-round, you can probably enjoy this activity any time of the year. If not, you may be only able to do this experiment in the spring, summer, or early fall.

MATERIALS:

Camera or phone (to take photos)

Wildflower iden-tification book or the Internet

Pencil

Markers, crayons, and/ or colored pencils

INSTRUCTIONS:

1. Go outside and take pictures of wildflowers. Try to find at least five different types of wildflowers.

2. Use a wildflower identification book or the Internet to try to figure out the name of each flower you found. You might need an adult's help with this part. To search online, type "wildflower identification online" for some great results!

3. Once you've identified your flowers, decide which one is your favorite. Write the name of it in the box on the next page, and draw a pic-ture of it. Make sure to add color.

4. Lastly, write three things that you like about this wildflower.

NAME OF FLOWER:	THREE THINGS I LIKE ABOUT THIS FLOWER:
	1.
	2.
	3.

PARENT CORNER: This memorable experiential activity is a fun way for your child to explore the world around them. If you have family or friends who live in different states, ask them to send your child pictures of wildflowers from their locations. Then ask your child to compare the new flowers to theirs. Are they the same or different? Talk about why you think that is.

Make a Plant Grow

Description: In this experiment, you will investigate what a plant needs to grow. Does it need shade, or does it need sun? Can a plant grow without water? It won't take long to set up this experiment, but it will take a little over two weeks to complete it. You will need to be patient, but it will be very exciting when your plants start to grow. It's a good idea to do this experiment outside.

MATERIALS:

Permanent marker or something else to label the cups

4 plastic cups

Potting soil

Small pack of seeds of your choice

Water

INSTRUCTIONS:

1. Have an adult use a permanent marker to label each cup:

   - Sun + Water
   - Shade + Water
   - Sun + No Water
   - Shade + No Water

2. Put soil into each cup so it is about two-thirds full.

3. Add 2 to 3 seeds into each cup.

4. Sprinkle a small amount of soil into each cup to cover the seeds.

5. Add just a little water to the cups that are labeled "Sun + Water" and "Shade + Water."

6. Find a good spot in your house that gets sun for at least a few hours a day. Put the "Sun + Water" and "Sun + No Water" cups in that spot.

7. Put the other two cups, "Shade + Water" and Shade + No Water," in a place that gets no sunlight at all. A pantry, closet, or even a cabinet would work well.

8. Every other day, put a little water in the cups labeled "Sun + Water" and "Shade + Water." As you water the plants, notice how the plants are doing. Has anything changed?

9. At the end of the two weeks, bring all the plants together and study them. Which ones grew the most? Were there any that didn't grow at all? Why do you think that is?

10. Use your observations to draw a conclusion about what makes a plant grow. Does it need sunlight or shade? Water or no water?

PARENT CORNER: This experiment is a great way to get your child to visualize plant growth and the factors that affect it. Once your child has drawn conclusions about what a plant needs to grow, they may have other ideas or questions. If you still have some left-over materials, let them explore and try other things to see if they impact plant growth.

Watercolor Flowers

Description: You probably know that plants need water to stay alive. Even when they are cut, flowers need water to stay pretty. But do you know what exactly happens when a flower is put into water? For this experiment you're going to see what happens.

MATERIALS:

Water

Clear plastic cup(s) or mason jars (one for each color you want to test)

Food coloring (any colors of your choice); 3 to 5 different colors is a good place to start

White carnations (2 or 3 for each color you want to test)

Scissors*

INSTRUCTIONS:

1. Put water into each cup so it's three-quarters full.

2. Add 7 to 10 drops of food coloring to each cup.

3. Have an adult cut the bottom of each flower stem at a slight angle.

4. Place 2 to 3 flowers in each cup.

5. Take what you already know about flowers and plants and make a hypothesis—guess what you think will happen to the plant and the water. Talk about your hypothesis with an adult.

6. Check on your flowers a few minutes after you placed them in the water. Then check in a few hours. And then check the next day. What happens to the flowers?

7. Talk with an adult about what happened in this experiment.

Caution: An adult should handle the scissors and do the cutting for this project.

PARENT CORNER: This experiment clearly shows how flower stems take water up to their petals. It might be beneficial to discuss the difference between a plant with roots and a cut flower. A plant with roots takes water in from the roots, then moves it up the stem. A cut flower doesn't have roots anymore, but it's still able to absorb water through the stem.

Magnet Mission

Description: You probably know that magnets stick to the refrigerator, but what other things do they stick to? In this experiment, you will investigate which things around your house are magnetic, or stick to the magnet, and which things aren't. Note: *Do not test things like credit cards, phones, or other electronic devices. They are not magnet-safe, and can be damaged with a magnet.*

MATERIALS:

Strong refrigerator magnets

5 to 10 household objects

INSTRUCTIONS:

1. For each object, hold the magnet in one hand and the object in the other. Bring the magnet close to the object to see if they bond, or stick together.

2. Observe which objects stick to the magnet and which don't. The items that stick to the magnet are "magnetic."

3. Compare the magnetic objects to one another. Do they all have something in common that makes them magnetic?

4. Compare the nonmagnetic objects to one another. Why do you think these objects are not magnetic?

PARENT CORNER: This hands-on inquiry activity encourages your child to construct their own understanding of magnetism. Although they may not know the exact terms related to magnetism, they'll connect their observations to build a strong understanding and baseline for further inquiry and learning on this topic in the future.

Sink or Float?

Description: Boats float on water and rocks sink. Do you know what other things sink or float? Let's experiment with things around the house. Collect 5 to 10 waterproof objects. Make sure you collect things that are all different shapes, sizes, and weights. The objects can be from nature, like rocks and leaves*; objects from the kitchen, like forks and spoons; and even some of your small toys—as long as they are water-safe! If you're unsure if something is waterproof, ask a parent. Then we'll use that data, or information, to make conclusions about why something either sinks or floats!

MATERIALS:

Shallow pan or large glass dish/container

Water

5 to 10 waterproof objects

Pencil

INSTRUCTIONS:

1. Fill a shallow pan or dish/container with some water.

2. One at a time, gently place each object in the water and observe what happens to it.

3. Fill in the chart on the next page with what you observe. Write the names of objects that sink in the "Sink" column and the objects that float in the "Float" column.

4. Look at the objects that sank. Do they have anything in common with one another?

5. Look at the objects that floated. Do they have anything in common with one another?

6. Compare the two groups, and see if you can figure out differences between the two. Why did some objects sink while others floated?

Caution: Always check with an adult before picking up leaves. Some plants have thorns or are poisonous.

SINK	FLOAT

Build a Buoyant Boat

Description: Now that you have a good idea of why things sink or float, let's put your knowledge to the test. Your job is to build a boat that is buoyant. This means it floats! To do this activity, think about what you know about boats already, or have an adult help you explore some images online. Then use those things to inspire your own mini boat creation.

MATERIALS:

Aluminum foil

Shallow pan or bathtub*

Water

Optional: pennies or other small waterproof objects

INSTRUCTIONS:

1. Have an adult pull out a piece of aluminum foil that is big enough for you to work with.

2. Create your boat from the foil and keep in mind that it can't have any holes in the bottom or water will get in.

3. Fill a shallow pan or bathtub with some water.

4. Place your boat into the water. Does it float?

5. Gently place waterproof objects into your boat one at a time and observe what happens. Does is stay afloat?

Caution: An adult should supervise if you're using the bathtub.

PARENT CORNER: This creative activity shares the concepts of buoyancy and gravity in a simple, visually engaging way. Although your child may not have learned about these concepts and terms yet, this experiment will help build an understanding of them. This activity is perfect for a little inventor, or for the child who loves to create things!

Let's Make Ice Cream!

Description: Is there anything better than ice cream? How about home-made ice cream? In this experiment, you're going to turn a liquid (milk) into a solid. The result will be yummy ice cream!

MATERIALS:

Measuring cups and spoons

1 cup whole milk

1 teaspoon vanilla extract

2 tablespoons sugar

1 quart-size zip-top plastic bag

1 gallon-size zip-top plastic bag

About 4 cups ice

¼ cup salt

Gloves or a towel

Bowl(s)

Spoon(s)

Optional: ice-cream toppings, such as sprinkles or chocolate chips

INSTRUCTIONS:

1. Measure the milk, vanilla, and sugar and pour each item into the quart-size bag.

2. Have an adult help you get all the air out of the bag and seal it tightly shut. Then gently squish the bag a bit to mix the ingredients.

3. Fill the gallon-size bag halfway with ice. Then add the salt and shake the bag to mix.

4. Put your quart-size bag inside the gallon bag with the ice and add a little more ice. Seal the gallon bag tightly.

5. Put on gloves or wrap the bag in a towel to protect your hands from the cold. Then shake the bag! Continue shaking for about 8 to 10 minutes. You should start noticing the milk getting thicker.

6. Once the ice cream has formed, take the quart bag out of the gallon bag. Use a spoon to mix up the ice cream.

7. Serve the ice cream in bowls or eat it right out of the bag! You can even add toppings like sprinkles.

PARENT CORNER: This classic STEM activity illustrates chemistry and states of matter in a fun and engaging way. When your child actively participates and watches the changes happen right in front of their eyes, they will be excited about the science involved. Eating the experiment afterward will only make this activity more engaging and interesting! Additionally, if your child participates in measuring the ingredients, they will sharpen their math skills and become more familiar with fractions.

Melting Matter

Description: In the scientific world, *matter* is the word for all the materials around us. Water is a type of matter. We know that water can be a liquid (water), a solid (ice), or a gas (water vapor). We also know that we can turn water into a solid by putting it in the freezer where it becomes ice. But, once we have ice, how can we turn it back into a liquid? In this experiment, you will try different methods of speeding up the solid-to-liquid process—by melting ice cubes.

MATERIALS:

Pencil

Ice cubes

Bowl

Timer

INSTRUCTIONS:

1. Make a hypothesis: What are things you can do to speed up the process of turning the ice into water? Write those ideas, called methods, in the table on the next page.

2. For each experiment, place your ice in a bowl and apply your method. Use a timer to figure out how long each ice cube takes to melt.

3. Write the results in the table on the next page.

4. When you've tried all your methods, talk with an adult about your findings. What changed ice to liquid the fastest? The slowest? Why might this be?

METHOD	TOTAL TIME IT TOOK TO GO FROM SOLID TO LIQUID

PARENT CORNER: This experiment is a concrete and visual way to introduce your child to states of matter and what causes changes in matter. It is a great prerequisite to the following activity, which creates a less-visible change from liquid to gas, and the activity after that, which explores a way to speed up the freezing process.

Microwaving Marshmallows

Description: This mystery experiment involves just two things—a marshmallow and a microwave. In this activity, you will see what happens to a marshmallow when you heat it up. The results may be shocking! Marshmallows are mostly made of sugar, water, and air. What do you think is going to happen?

MATERIALS:

Marshmallow(s)

Microwave-safe plate

INSTRUCTIONS:

1. Place one marshmallow in the middle of the plate.

2. Ask an adult to place the plate in the microwave and set the microwave for 30 seconds. Before you start the microwave, make a prediction. What do you think will happen to the marshmallow?

3. After the 30 seconds, ask an adult to take the marshmallow out of the microwave.

4. What happened to the marshmallow? Keep observing to see if it changes.

5. What happens when it cools down?

6. Repeat this experiment with other marshmallows, but keep them in the microwave for shorter or longer amounts of time.

PARENT CORNER: The science behind this experiment is a little complex. The liquids in the marshmallow turn into gas and expand as it heats up. It illustrates another matter change (liquid to gas), but in a less-obvious way. If your child has experience with heating marshmallows over a fire to make smores, connect this experiment to that experience. Ask them to think about what happens to a marshmallow when it's heated in the fire versus what happens when it's heated in the microwave. Ask if the result is the same or different, and why that may be.

Gifted and Talented Workbook for Kids

Crystal Creator

Description: Crystals are everywhere in nature. Diamonds, sugar, and even snowflakes are all crystals. With a few simple ingredients and a little bit of patience, you can create crystals in your very own home.

MATERIALS:

Measuring cups

1 cup water

Mason jar

¼ cup borax

Spoon

Pipe cleaner

Ice-pop stick

INSTRUCTIONS:

1. Have an adult boil 1 cup of water in the microwave or on the stove.

2. Have an adult pour the boiling water into the mason jar.

3. Measure and add ¼ cup of borax to the jar.

4. Carefully stir the mixture until the borax is completely dissolved. Be careful! The jar is hot!

5. Twist one end of the pipe cleaner around the middle section of ice-pop stick. The pipe cleaner should be hanging down off the stick.

6. Place the ice-pop stick across the top of the jar so the pipe cleaner hangs inside. If it touches the bottom of the jar, twist more of the pipe cleaner around the stick to make it shorter.

7. Now it's time to be patient. It will take about 24 to 48 hours for your crystals to form.

8. Keep an eye on the jar to see the crystals forming, but don't pick it up. Keep the jar completely still. After 48 hours, gently lift up the ice-pop stick and observe the crystals you created.

Caution: Never ingest borax.

PARENT CORNER: This magical experiment introduces your child to supersaturation. Hot water can hold more powder than cold water. As the water cools, the extra borax powder separates from the water and begins to form crystals. Your child might be too young to understand the scientific explanations, but they can still enjoy this memorable experiment.

Go Away Monster Spray

Description: Today, you will make a special spray that will make monsters go away. This spray smells good and will make monsters feel calm and relaxed, so they won't come in your room.

MATERIALS:

Empty spray bottle

Water

Lavender essential oil or other lavender liquid fragrance

Optional: stickers

INSTRUCTIONS:

1. Fill your spray bottle three-quarters of the way with water.

2. Add 2 or 3 drops of the magic ingredient (lavender oil) that will scare all the monsters away.

3. Put the lid on the spray bottle and gently shake it to combine all the ingredients.

4. Decorate your spray bottle with stickers if you would like.

5. Next time you detect a monster, use your bottle. Two to three sprays should do the trick! This works especially well for getting rid of monsters under your bed and in your closet.

PARENT CORNER: Gifted children tend to lean toward being more anxious because they're usually more aware of everything that's going on around them. This monster spray is a fun and easy way to put their mind at ease. Provide context and an explanation for why it will work to make the benefits of this spray plausible for even the most skeptical child.

Egg Drop

Description: Think about how delicate eggs can be. With this experiment, you'll have the chance to create the ultimate protection for a raw egg. Your mission is to create a contraption, using household items, that will protect an egg when it is dropped from a height of about 10 feet.

MATERIALS:

Some or all of the following materials:

- Bubble wrap
- Tissue paper
- Newspaper
- Plastic bag(s)
- String
- Anything else you think will protect an egg

Small to medium cardboard box

Scissors

Raw eggs

Packing tape or masking tape

Plastic zip-top sandwich bag

INSTRUCTIONS:

1. Look at the ideas on the materials list and think of what you want to put in a cardboard box.

2. Collect your materials and think about how this should be done. Begin creating your contraption that will protect your egg.

3. Once you're satisfied with your contraption, set it aside. Put a raw egg in a plastic bag and zip it shut. Put the egg into your box with anything else you want to use and tape it shut.

4. Ask an adult to drop your contraption from about 10 feet off the ground on the ground. Don't drop it on grass because it's soft and will absorb the impact of the fall.

5. Open the box to see if the egg survived the fall. If it did, congratulations! If not, try to figure out why the egg broke and try a new contraption that you think will work even better.

PARENT CORNER: This classic STEM activity introduces the concept of gravity. Once your child has a contraption that protects the egg, drop it from a higher height and see if it still protects the egg. If not, talk about why this might be. If they succeed, try for a third time from an even higher level.

Lighter and Heavier

Description: This fun experiment uses gravity to compare the weights of different objects so that you can see which is heavier. First, you will need to make a balancing scale. Then you will use it to compare the weights of any small objects you want to test!

MATERIALS:

2 plastic cups

Hole punch or something sharp to poke holes in the plastic cups

String

Scissors

Plastic clothes hanger that has notches on the top edge

Small objects that will fit in the plastic cups

INSTRUCTIONS:

1. Ask an adult to poke two holes across from each other and below the rim of each cup.

2. Then ask an adult to cut two pieces of string that are each about a foot long.

3. Put the string through the first hole and tie a knot to keep it in place. Put the other end of the string through the other hole and tie that, too. You should have something that looks like a bucket handle. Repeat this step with the second cup.

4. Hang one cup in the top notch on each side of the hanger.

5. Hook the hanger somewhere it can hang freely. A doorknob is a good place.

6. Now it's time to experiment. Put different objects in each cup to see which is heaviest. Hint: The cup that is lower is the heavier cup!

PARENT CORNER: This hands-on activity incorporates the law of gravity in a concrete and visual way. Some children may not know the term *gravity*, but they'll start to see how it works while using this balance scale. For an extra challenge, encourage your child to figure out how to make the scale completely balanced or both sides equal in weight.

Chapter 1: Language Arts

Picture to Word Search - page 7

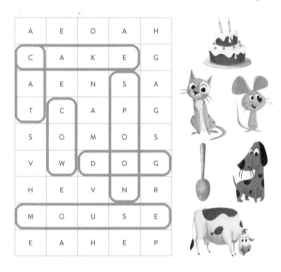

Tall, Taller, Tallest - page 9

Taller   Tallest   Tall

Everyday Emotions - page 13

Mad/Angry   Surprised   Happy

Shy   Sad/Thoughtful   Silly

Answers may vary.

It's Rhyme Time - page 21

WORD ONE	WORD TWO	DO THEY RHYME? YES / NO
Cat	Hat	YES
Muffin	Puffin	YES
Drill	Drum	NO
Jewel	Cool	YES

Verb, Noun, or Neither? - page 22

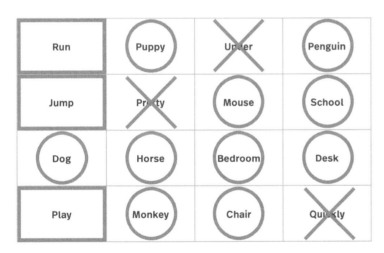

What Comes Next? - page 26

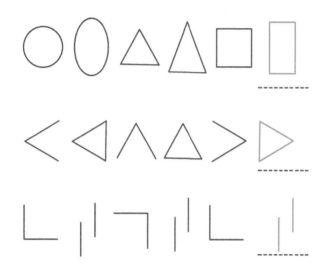

Pattern Perfector - page 29

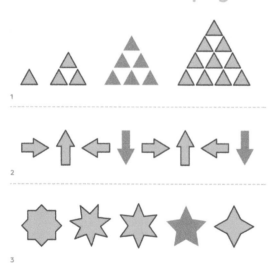

Peter's Pattern Problem - page 30

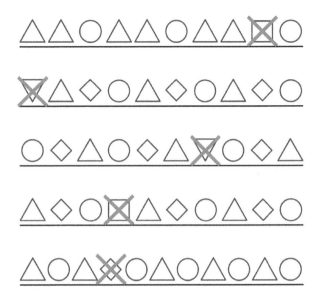

Max's Car Collection - page 31

There are two possible answers:

Green, Orange, Red, Yellow, Blue

Blue, Orange, Red, Yellow, Green

Super School Subjects - page 32

	MATH	READING	SCIENCE
Jessica	X	✓	X
Jamal	X	X	✓
Jeremy	✓	X	X

How Many Birthday Candles? - page 33

	5	6	7
Maggie	X	✓	X
Miguel	X	X	✓
Micah	✓	X	X

Shape Sudoku 1 - page 34

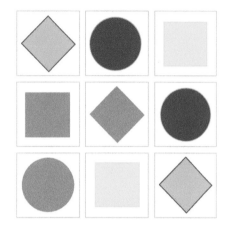

Shape Sudoku 2 - page 35

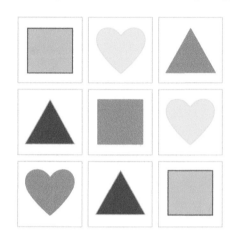

Number Sudoku 1 - page 36

3	1	2
1	2	3
2	3	1

Number Sudoku 2 - page 37

1	3	2
3	2	1
2	1	3

Picture Analogies - page 38

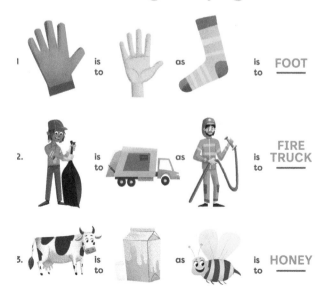

1   is to   as   is to   FOOT

2.   is to   as   is to   FIRE TRUCK

3.   is to   as   is to   HONEY

Shape Story - page 39

Word Connection - page 40

Fish	**is to**	Swim	**as**	Snake	**is to**	Slither
Summer	**is to**	Flip Flops	**as**	Winter	**is to**	Snow Boots (or just boots)
Apple	**is to**	Tree	**as**	Carrot	**is to**	Groud (or under-ground)

Shape Sleuth - page 41

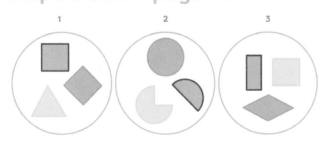

WHAT DO THESE SHAPES HAVE IN COMMON?	WHAT DO THESE SHAPES HAVE IN COMMON?	WHAT DO THESE SHAPES HAVE IN COMMON?
Each shape has sides that are all the same length	Each shape has at least one side that is rounded	Each shape has 4 sides

Which Doesn't Belong? - page 43

Add One More - page 44

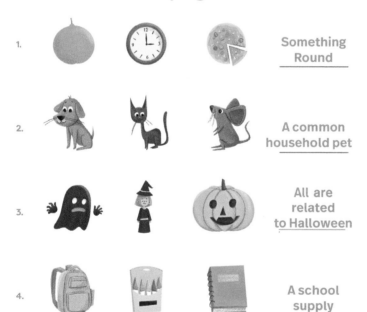

1. Something Round
2. A common household pet
3. All are related to Halloween
4. A school supply

Across and Down - page 45

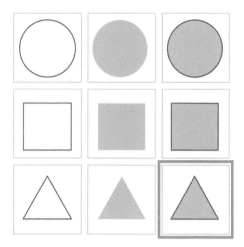

Cause and Effect - page 46

CAUSE	EFFECT
A child is slowly eating an ice-cream cone in the sun on a hot day.	The ice cream melts.
It's likely that Zack eats too much candy and/or doesn't brush his teeth.	Zack has three cavities.
Krista forgot her lunch at home.	It's likely that Krista was hungry at school *or* had to buy school lunch. Maybe her mom had to bring her lunch?
Nobody watered the plant *or* the plant didn't get enough sun *or* any other plausible cause.	The plant dies.

Chapter 3: Math

Adding Shapes - page 50

♥ ♥ ♥ + ♥ ♥ = <u>5</u>

♥ ♥ ♥ ♥ + ♡♡ = <u>6</u>

♡♡♡♡♡ + ♡♡♡♡♡ = <u>10</u>

<u>Answers may vary.</u> + _____ = __

Addition Detective - page 51

5 + <u>3</u> = 8

<u>3</u> + 6 = 9

4 + <u>2</u> = 6

<u>0</u> + 10 = 10

7 + <u>2</u> = 9

<u>3</u> + 2 = 5

1 + <u>6</u> = 7

Subtraction Situation - page 52

<u>10</u> – 2 = 8

<u>10</u> – 10 = 0

6 – <u>4</u> = 2

<u>9</u> – 5 = 4

5 – <u>2</u> = 3

10 – <u>1</u> = 9

<u>10</u> – 3 = 7

More and Less - page 53

1

	10 less 15	
1 less 24	**25**	1 more 26
	35 10 more	

2

	10 less 20	
1 less 29	**30**	1 more 31
	40 10 more	

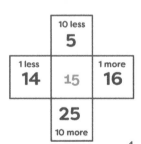

3

	10 less 0	
1 less 9	10	1 more 11
	20 10 more	

4

	10 less 5	
1 less 14	15	1 more 16
	25 10 more	

Puppy, Please! - page 54

Melissa doesn't have enough money yet because she only has 60 cents, which is less than 95 cents.

Blooming Math Flowers - page 55

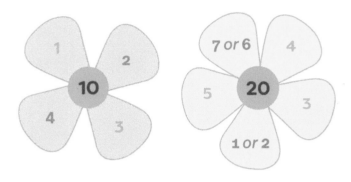

Three Squares - page 56

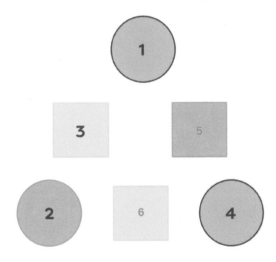

Pyramid Puzzle - page 57

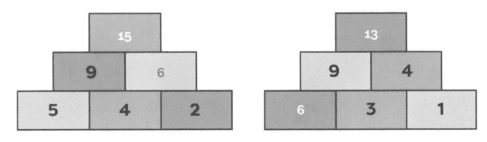

Completing Carla's Patterns - page 58

1, 2, 3, <u>4</u>, <u>5</u>, <u>6</u>

5, 10, 15, <u>20</u>, <u>25</u>, <u>30</u>

2, 4, 6, <u>8</u>, <u>10</u>, <u>12</u>

6, 8, 10, <u>12</u>, <u>14</u>, <u>16</u>

8, 11, 14, <u>17</u>, <u>20</u>, <u>23</u>

Martin's Missing Numbers - page 59

1, 3, 5, <u>7</u>, 9 <u>11</u>

3, 6, <u>9</u>, 12, <u>15</u>

10, 12, <u>14</u>, 16, <u>18</u>

0, 5, <u>10</u>, <u>15</u>, 20, 25

4, <u>8</u>, 12, 16, <u>20</u>, <u>24</u>

Dominic's Dominoes - page 60

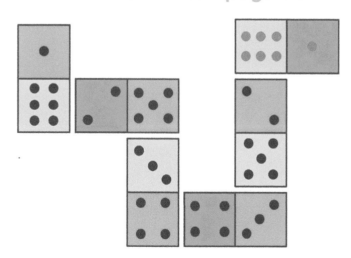

Shape Search - page 63

Circles = 1

Triangles = 8

Squares = 1

Rectangles = 3

Butterfly Wings - page 65

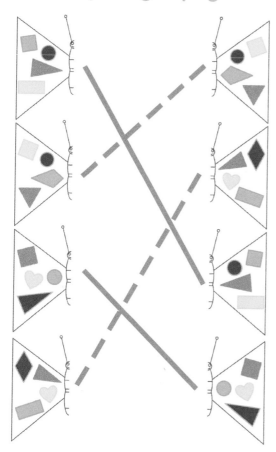

Piece of Cake - page 67

Answers may vary; however, the goal is for the child to realize that either option is actually the same amount of cake.

Tricky Triangle Challenge - page 68

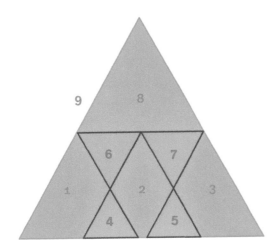

9 triangles

How Many on the Bus? - page 69

The total number of kids that are still on the bus is 0.

Resources

Book for kids, especially those that tend to lean toward perfectionism: *The Girl Who Never Made Mistakes* by Mark Pett and Gary Rubinstein

Book for parents: *Parenting Gifted Kids: Tips for Raising Happy and Successful Gifted Children* by James Delisle

Book for parents: *Smart Parenting for Smart Kids: Nurturing Your Child's True Potential* by Eileen Kennedy-Moore and Mark S. Lowenthal

Byrdseed—Byrdseed.com

Gifted Guru—GiftedGuru.com

Free online sudoku puzzles—1sudoku.com

The Maker Mom: Helping parents raise STEM-loving, Maker-friendly kids—TheMakerMom.com /gifted-kids

Mensa for Kids—MensaForKids.org

National Association for Gifted Children—NAGC.org

NASA all about the moon—Moon.NASA.gov

Wonderopolis—Wonderopolis.com

References

Congress of the United States. "Elementary and Secondary Education Act of 1965." April 11, 1965. https://eric.ed.gov/?id=ED017539.

Office for Civil Rights, US Department of Education. "Civil Rights Data Collection." Accessed March 3, 2021. https://ocrdata.ed.gov/estimations/2015-2016.

Acknowledgments

A special thanks to my parents for their love, support, and encouragement in everything I do. Thank you for encouraging me to find and follow my passion, and for supporting me in making my dream of becoming a teacher a reality.

I also want to thank my grandparents for constantly supporting me, believing in me, and showing me what I want to become when I grow up. Through weekly FaceTime and phone calls to check in, your support means the world to me.

Thank you to my teacher friends for celebrating the teacher wins with me, helping me conquer the challenges, and encouraging me in my teacherpreneur endeavors. It's thanks to each one of you that I have grown to become both a better teacher and a better person.

And, last but not least, thank you to Callisto Media for believing in me, and to everyone on the team who worked tirelessly to make this book a reality. I couldn't have done it without each and every one of you.

About the Author

Rachel Martino, MEd, is an advanced academics specialist and teacher of the Gifted and Talented who has spent her entire career focused on educating and serving the gifted population. Founder of InsideTheGiftedClassroom.com, Rachel is passionate about creating resources to help all educators meet the needs of the gifted students in their classroom. Rachel hopes that this book will inspire and challenge young learners, while empowering their parents with information, tips, and resources to best support their gifted child. In her free time, Rachel loves to read, paint, and spend time with her family.

CPSIA information can be obtained
at www.ICGtesting.com
Printed in the USA
JSHW010240300122
22388JS00007B/9